Word Memory Power in 30 Days

Word Memory Power in 30 Days

PETER FUNK

with

BARRY TARSHIS

Beekman House/New York

This 1986 edition is published by Beekman House, distributed by
Crown Publishers, Inc., by arrangement with Delacorte Press

Printed and Bound in the United States of America

Library of Congress Cataloging-in-Publication Data

Funk, Peter, 1921–
  Word memory power in 30 days.

  Reprint. Originally published: New York, N.Y. : Delacorte Press,
c1981.
  Includes index.
  1. Vocabulary. I. Tarshis, Barry. II. Title.
PE1449.F77   1986   428.1   86-3501
ISBN 0-517-60363-2

h g f e d c b a

To you the reader,
who we hope will enjoy using this
book as much as we enjoyed creating it.

Mary Funk was involved in such a multiplicity of activities on this project, it is difficult to know where to begin and end the list. Our grateful thanks to her for her enthusiasm and expertise.

CONTENTS

Word Memory Power in 30 Days

What Was That Word Again?

Despite the popularity of vocabulary-building books, a great many people have difficulty remembering the words they learn while reading these books. As a linguist writing the monthly <u>Reader's Digest</u> feature "It Pays to Enrich Your Word Power," I find the plight almost universal—even among people with advanced degrees.

The problem nagged me for a long while. But I believe that in this book I have found a new way to help you remember words more easily than you have ever done before.

People today recognize the value of a solid and varied vocabulary. Innumerable studies in recent years show beyond a doubt that a strong vocabulary helps you do better in school, in business, and in the professions. The right words are often as pivotal in successful negotiations as they are in your daily relationships. People who have developed a large "mental dictionary" have more confidence and certainly derive more pleasure from reading, as well as from movies and television.

Like other linguists, I have relied on a variety of games and quizzes in my previous books and in my column to help readers remember words and learn how to use them accurately. The approach was pioneered by my father, Wilfred Funk, more than forty years ago. This technique is as valid as it ever was and should be an integral part of any serious program of vocabulary improvement. In fact such games and quizzes make up a part of this book.

But such an approach is only a partial answer to word memory. The common experience for most people is that many of the new words they learn slip out of their memories all too quickly. I knew something else was needed. But what?

One day an editor suggested I write a vocabulary builder based on the latest mnemonic or memory techniques. And this is what I've done. As far as I know, <u>Word Memory Power in 30 Days</u> is the first book that integrates mnemonic (pronounced nee MON ik) techniques into a definite strategy for building the kind of vocabulary you'd like to have. Mnemonics, as you may know already, refers to the science or art of memory improvement through the use of certain devices.

The beauty of the system I use is its simplicity. You can apply it to any new word you learn. Later on in this section I'll explain how you can put these techniques to work for you.

First, however, I want to tell you a little something about the 200-plus words you'll be working with. All of them should be in your verbal arsenal. They cover a broad spectrum of subjects and are loosely grouped under a variety of topics.

These important words impinge on your daily life—sometimes directly and dramatically, sometimes subtly. They involve the concepts, ideas, and expressions that are influential in shaping the quality of your life.

They are "everyday" words. That's the way I like to think of them. They are "everyday" in the sense that you're likely to come on them as you read, when you listen to people talk, or when you hear them on the radio and TV. None of them is esoteric or dated.

All of them, of course, can be looked up in any good dictionary. But dictionaries have one failing. As necessary as they are, they don't have the space to give you a full picture of a word and most of the time you get only the bare bones.

That's why I've explored each of them in some depth, giving you their backgrounds, showing you how they are used and misused today. At the end of each cluster of five chapters you will have an opportunity to test yourself as to how well you know each of the words you've covered. Though the book has a scholarly base, I believe you will find it entertaining to read and easy to use.

You may have noticed that the book is divided into four weeks, which explains the title Word Memory Power in 30 Days. Then, so as to give you a certain number of words each day, each week is divided into five days. You have the weekend off for review to catch up for any day you may have missed. An arrangement like this allows you a certain flexibility, making it easier for you to lay out a program of study. There's no great mystery in learning something new. It's a matter of keeping after it on a fairly regular basis. At the end of thirty days, I'm sure you're going to be surprised and delighted at how many of the new words have seeped into your working vocabulary.

Mnemonics and Word Memory

A mnemonic device is an artificial contrivance to help your memory. We've all used mnemonic devices consciously or unconsciously at one time or another. Chances are, when you were in grade school, a teacher gave you a little tip to assist you to keep in mind the spelling of a certain word. You remembered to put the i before e in the word <u>piece</u> by thinking of the phrase a "piece of pie."

I know people who routinely use mnemonic devices to recall the names of people. You meet a man named Harry who has a ton of hair, and you think, <u>Hairy Harry.</u> Another man I know keeps the nautical terms <u>port</u> and <u>starboard</u> straight by using the question "Is there any port <u>left</u> in the wine cabinet?"

Different as each of these mnemonic devices may be, they all represent the same basic concept: association. You associate, or connect, whatever you want to remember with something already familiar to you, or something easier to recall than the original object to be remembered.

Since relatively little is known about the mechanics of memory (although there is some fascinating research going on in the field), no one really understands the processes that make mnemonic devices work. But an abundance of studies show that they do work and that is what's important for you and me to know.

There are different types of memory: long-term and short-term. An apparently effective way of converting easily forgotten short-term memory into the more enduring long-term one is to make a connection between the two: that is, connect a new piece of information with information already stored in long-term memory.

The mnemonic devices accompanying each of the words in this book create an association to help you remember the word. But remembering is not the same thing as mastering. The individual word descriptions explain clearly and fully just about all you will want to know about that word. That part has nothing to do with mnemonics.

You may find it tempting at times to skim over the word description, concentrating on the mnemonic device. I urge you not to. What is particularly useful about the mnemonic system is that it doesn't discard the traditional methods of vocabulary building. It simply adds to these methods a new and enjoyable way of imprinting a word more permanently in your memory, which is what you want.

I'd like you to keep in mind that using the mnemonic devices in this book is very much a game—a game, moreover, in which there are no rigid rules, a game governed by common sense and imagination.

For example, take cryptic, a word you'll be working with in the book. Cryptic is an adjective that conveys the idea of having a hidden meaning. The word description explains all of this and shows you how the word can be used.

Following this description is a word which I call the word link. The word link is a word or a phrase that sums up the essence of the word's meaning. With cryptic, the word link is hidden. This is the link between the meaning of the word and the device that's going to glue it in your memory.

Now to the mnemonic device. The idea is to come up with an association that will link cryptic with hidden. Most of the time I've used a play on words. What does cryptic (KRIP tick) sound like? Can we come up with an image based on the sound—not the meaning—of the word? <u>Cryptic.</u> Say it enough times and maybe you'll hear the phrase <u>crib tick</u> as I did.

Now, if you let your mind play with the sound, a <u>crib</u> is easy. What about <u>tick</u>? What if there was a clock in the crib? A clock <u>hidden</u> in the crib makes it seem as if the CRIB is TICKing (CRYP-TIC).

Let's try another—<u>kowtow.</u> The word means "to fawn over, to defer to in a servile way." When you kowtow to somebody, you are, figuratively speaking, bowing down to him. Here again, the word description provides you with a good background on the word. My word link is <u>bend over.</u> It catches the spirit of the word.

Here, as with <u>cryptic,</u> a play on words does the trick. Doesn't kowtow sound like cow toe? And if you want to see a cow toe what do you do? Bend over, of course. So here you have the link between kowtow and bend over.

This method of recalling a word helps you to have it on hand whenever you want, so that later you won't be saying to yourself, "That's the word I meant to use. Why couldn't I remember it?"

A moment's glance at any one of the words in this book will probably clear up most questions you have about the process. Each word has both a word link and a memory key that you won't have any difficulty using. If you don't like the ones I've made up, create your own devices.

You can relate words to people you know, or to phrases or names very familiar to you. You can make up funny scenes in your head. The more absurd the imagined situation, incidentally, the more impact the image will have and the better will be the retention power of the device. Play around with words. The trick is to let go. Let your imagination fly. Have fun. You have an unlimited license in your use of mnemonic devices. You can even be earthy. Who's going to know?

One final word: I'm enthusiastic about the possibilities of what <u>Word Memory Power in 30 Days</u> can do for you. By the time you finish this book, several things will have happened.

You will have increased your vocabulary substantially, and will have an enviable expertise in understanding and knowing how to handle these mainspring words. At the same time, you will find yourself far better acquainted with hundreds and hundreds of related words. You will have added to your word supply dramatically, and you will have learned new ways to remember words more easily and permanently.

But above all, my real hope is that because of this breakthrough in word memory techniques, you will be stimulated to continue adding to your store of words.

Even though you have a strong and active mind, until you build a comparably vigorous vocabulary you can use effectively, your mind will never develop its potential. I believe my book will help you toward this goal and bring you new enjoyment and success in every area of your life, for new words express new life.

Verbs That Pack a Punch

Want to make a "hit"? Use verbs that pack a punch—ones needing no adverb to get their message across. You're right if you hesitate to flaunt your burgeoning vocabulary. But don't be shy about using it freely to substantiate your word memory power. And by the way, you can be sure no one's going to dare malign your verbal skills when they know you can inundate a heckler with power words.

badger
malign
rescind
flaunt
cavil
wreak
burgeon
inundate
subvert
substantiate

BADGER
(BAJ ur)—to harass, pester, or nag

One of the delights of language is that sometimes a single word such as BADGER resembles a microfilm, for it compresses into a small space a story or a full description of an incident. Many years ago in Europe and America, a popular entertainment was badger baiting. Badgers, small and fierce animals, were placed into a hole or barrel where they could neither escape nor adequately defend themselves against dogs who were trained to torment them. This cruel sport gave us our word BADGER.

We use the word today to describe an action whose purpose is to pester or torment somebody else. Perhaps in a legal drama on TV you've seen a lawyer BADGERING a witness in court. And an exasperated stockbroker told me of a client who BADGERS him for the kind of stocks that only go up and never down.

Word Link: HARASS

Memory Key: A BAD YEAR (BADGER) can HARASS a wine maker trying to build a reputation.

MALIGN
(muh LINE)—to slander; say harmful untruths about

To MALIGN someone is to say or write something deliberately intended to hurt that person's reputation. Generally, when we use the word the implication is that the things being said or written are misleading and untrue. The key isn't so much what's being said as the motivation behind the statement. If you have proof that a politician has taken a bribe and you testify to the fact, you haven't MALIGNED his reputation. You would MALIGN, however, if you concocted a false story expressly for the purpose of discrediting him.

MALIGN, of course, is closely related to the adjective malignant, which is usually associated with cancer but can be used to convey the notion of something having a harmful effect.

Word Link: HURT

Memory Key: A MA LION (MALIGN) can HURT you more than a pa lion when she's defending her cubs.

RESCIND ==
(re SIND)—to revoke, cancel, annul, retract, or invalidate

The synonyms revoke, recall, retract, reverse, repeal, and RESCIND all have a similar meaning, "to cancel." It's interesting that each of them begins with the prefix re. This Latin prefix can mean "again" or, as with these words, "back."

Much of the time you can use revoke in place of RESCIND, though RESCIND is best confined to legal situations in which laws or rights have been canceled. When governments change radically, for instance, certain rights such as free speech, voting, etc., are frequently RESCINDED. There are times when local communities find it necessary to RESCIND laws that have been on the books for many years and no longer apply to present-day situations.

Word Link: CANCEL

Memory Key: Your flight to the city of RACINE (RESCIND), Wisconsin, has been CANCELED because of bad weather.

FLAUNT

—show off in an ostentatious way

Some years ago, an airline ran a campaign whose slogan was "When you've got it, FLAUNT it." The idea behind FLAUNT is to put on a boastful display, and the word should not be confused with the similar sounding flout, which means "to treat with scorn, disdain, or contempt." As it happens, the two words are frequently confused, and columnist William Safire once took former President Carter to task for misusing them. "You can flout convention," said Safire, "and you can flout authority, but you cannot use FLAUNT for flout." I like Professor Bergen Evans's way of clarifying the difference between the two words. "Someone who FLAUNTS unconventionality or immorality," points out Evans, "flouts the conventions or mores of the community."

Word Link: SHOW OFF

Memory Key: PHIL's AUNT (FLAUNT) is a SHOW-OFF.

CAVIL

(KAV il)—find fault without good reason; raise frivolous or picayune objections to; carp

We all know the type: the person who is constantly finding fault, quibbling over the most trivial points, endlessly raising petty objections. Such a person has a CAVILING nature. To qualify for this description, you have to do more than simply criticize or find fault with. You have to do so without any reason other than hostility or a desire to provoke trouble. It often happens during a tense labor negotiation that just when it seems as if there will be a breakthrough, one of the participants begins to CAVIL over an unimportant clause.

Word Link: CRITICIZE

Memory Key: The U.S. CAVALry (CAVIL) was CRITICIZED greatly after Custer's defeat at Little Big Horn.

WREAK
(REEK)—to inflict destruction; damage

The pithy vigor of this Old English word tells us something about the character of the fierce Northern Europeans of the Middle Ages whose plunderous conquests left a long and bloody trail of destruction and damage. This is a strong word often used in accounts of natural disasters, but it's also a word that may be suffering from overexposure. As an editor friend of mine once said to a young reporter, "Your description of a storm 'WREAKING havoc' on the residents of California <u>reeks</u> of overuse. It's a cliché."

Word Link: DAMAGE

Memory Key: A fire that causes great DAMAGE will REEK (WREAK) for hours.

BURGEON
(BUR jun)—to grow; flourish; develop; proliferate; sprout

To a horticulturist, the term BURGEONING means the growth of a plant as it puts out new shoots and buds, but the word can represent any flourishing growth, whether it be a city, a career, or a sport. Even love seems to BURGEON in a special way as soon as the first flowers of spring appear.

Word Link: GROW

Memory Key: The BIRDS YOU OWN (BURGEON) will GROW if you feed them well.

INUNDATE
(IN un date)—to flood; overwhelm

It's one thing to be busy but something else again to be INUN-DATED with work. INUNDATE is the word you use when you want to suggest the idea of being overwhelmed. If you've been in the Southwest during a cloudburst, you know how quickly a canyon can be INUNDATED with water. And every spring, it seems, the nightly television news shows us scenes of communities being INUNDATED by flood waters. Technically, the word is more at home in meteorological situations than anywhere else, but the figurative use of the word is becoming more and more accepted. I once heard a young girl say that she was INUNDATED by love.

Word Link: FLOOD

Memory Key: The NUN who went on a DATE (INUNDATE) caused a FLOOD of protests.

SUBVERT
(sub VERT)—to overthrow; ruin; corrupt

To SUBVERT is to work with the express notion of tearing down or corrupting a system or institution or philosophy that has long served as the foundation of people's lives. One of the principle causes of the Iranian revolution in 1979, for instance, was the fear among many Iranians that western influences were SUBVERTING the basic values and life-style of the Muslim faith. In many demo-cratic nations today, there is a growing fear of forces that might serve to SUBVERT the basic freedoms on which the governments of these nations are built. Such forces are usually described as subversive. This word has a Latin origin and comes from the word subvertere, which means, literally, "to underturn."

Word Link: OVERTHROW

Memory Key: An OVERTHROWN submarine could cause a condition called SUB VERTigo (SUBVERT).

SUBSTANTIATE

(sub STAN she ate)—to confirm; establish by proof of evidence; verify

SUBSTANTIATE is a sturdy word that stands firm. You can count on it. To SUBSTANTIATE a statement is to gather and present evidence that proves the statement is true. Scientists often spend years searching for the data to SUBSTANTIATE their hypothesis.

Two English words closely related to SUBSTANTIATE are substantial, meaning "solid or strong," and substantive, meaning "of a considerable amount or a major portion," as when a lawyer presents the substantive part of his argument.

Word Link: PROVE

Memory Key: The huge SUB SAND which SHE ATE (SUBSTANTIATE) PROVED how hungry she was.

Word Game I

Choose the correct answer from the multiple choices after each phrase:

1. To be <u>badgered</u> is to be
   A. flattered
   B. tormented
   C. made angry

2. One way of <u>maligning</u> somebody is to
   A. strike him in the face
   B. insult him
   C. spread a lie about him

3. You might describe a person who <u>flaunts</u> his wealth as a
   A. show-off
   B. tightwad
   C. spendthrift

4. To <u>cavil</u> at another person is to
   A. scold them
   B. find fault with them
   C. praise them

5. <u>Wreak</u> is a word you would normally associate with a
   A. library
   B. meal
   C. storm

6. A city that is <u>burgeoning</u> is
   A. losing population
   B. growing rapidly
   C. suffering from air pollution

7. If you were <u>inundated</u> with work, you would be
   A. very busy

B. not busy at all

C. irritated

8. A person who is out to <u>subvert</u> a plan of yours is somebody you should
   A. go to for help
   B. be wary of
   C. ignore

9. A person who <u>substantiated</u> a story you told is somebody who
   A. disagrees with the story
   B. supports the story with facts
   C. makes fun of the story

10. A law that has been <u>rescinded</u> is one that is
    A. no longer in effect
    B. stronger than ever before
    C. applicable only to certain people

Answers: 1-B 2-C 3-A 4-B 5-C 6-B 7-A 8-B 9-B 10-A

Word Game □□

Match the word in the left-hand column with the word in the right-hand column that has the closest association.

1. badger	A. boast
2. malign	B. flood
3. flaunt	C. authenticate
4. cavil	D. inflict
5. wreak	E. reputation
6. burgeon	F. burst forth
7. inundate	G. quibble
8. subvert	H. overturn
9. substantiate	I. nag
10. rescind	J. abolish

Answers: 1-I 2-E 3-A 4-G 5-D 6-F 7-B 8-H 9-C 10-J

Word Game ▯▯▯

Write in the word link next to the word and let your imagination see the memory link:

1. rescind _____

2. malign _____

3. substantiate _____

4. burgeon _____

5. flaunt _____

6. cavil _____

7. inundate _____

8. subvert _____

9. badger _____

10. wreak _____

Answers: 1. cancel 2. hurt 3. prove 4. grow 5. show off 6. criticize 7. flood 8. overthrow 9. harass 10. damage

Don't forget to review memory key images with word links.

IV

Laboratory Report

WEEK 1, DAY 2

Inside the laboratory, scientific words have very precise meanings. And well they must, given the demands of scientific inquiry. But once a scientific word works its way into general conversation, all bets are off.

Each of the words in this section has a specific scientific meaning, but take it out of the laboratory and you have license to use the word in any number of different ways. The ability to use scientific words figuratively gives your vocabulary added color and flexibility.

biodegradable
catalyst
galaxy
fossil
hybrid
clone
fission
synergism
binary
empirical

BIODEGRADABLE

(by oh die GRAY duh b'l)—able to decompose biologically into harmless products by bacterial action

BIODEGRADABLE is a hybrid of the Greek root bios, "life," and the Latin word degradere, "to reduce." The word is so new you won't find it in any dictionary published prior to 1970. An important word to environmentalists, BIODEGRADABLE was invented by modern scientists to distinguish substances that decompose biologically as part of nature (fruit, vegetables, paper, boxes, etc.) from substances that do not decompose naturally and hence serve to pollute the environment. It is now generally accepted that by making products out of BIODEGRADABLE materials, we could substantially reduce environmental pollution.

Word Link: DECOMPOSE

Memory Key: If you BUY A DIE molding tool that's GRATABLE (BIODEGRADABLE), you should be able to shred it. In other words, a DECOMPOSABLE die.

CATALYST

(CAT'l ist)—stimulus; a substance that accelerates a chemical reaction

If you know anything about chemistry, you understand that a CATALYTIC substance is one that activates or speeds up a chemical reaction without itself appearing to undergo any permanent change. Nickel, for instance, is used in the processing of margarine as a carrier of hydrogen, which is necessary in hardening the butter substitute. Outside the laboratory, the word conveys the same idea. I recall a high school teacher who was a prime CATALYST in sparking my interest in literature. He remained the same person, but I was changed for life.

Word Link: STIMULUS

Memory Key: The cow, seeing his name on the slaughterhouse CATTLE LIST (CATALYST), was STIMULATED to run away.

GALAXY ═══════════════════════════════════
(GAL ak see)—vast cluster of stars; also any brilliant group of people

One thrilling aspect of investigating word meanings is that we are exposed to areas that expand our minds. Learning, for example, that a GALAXY might include hundreds of billions of stars and be 300,000 light-years in diameter (light travels 180,000 miles a second) helps explain why many scientists describe the size of the universe as "incalculable."

But back to GALAXY. Its root is the Greek word, gala, "milk." Yes, this is the origin of the phrase "Milky Way," which refers to the luminous milky appearance of stars. But the word has a closer to earth definition and can be used, and unfortunately overused, to describe a gathering of brilliant, famous, or "beautiful" people.

Word Link: STAR

Memory Key: Now that he has a telescope, ALEX SEES (GALAXY) STARS every night.

FOSSIL ═══════════════════════════════════
(FOSS'l)—plant or animal remains preserved in the earth

Not long ago in Egypt scientists discovered FOSSILIZED bits of a skeleton of a monkey thought to be 30 million years old and possibly the oldest common ancestor of apes and men. The fact that the bones were FOSSILIZED meant they were the remains of life from a much earlier age preserved in the earth. That's the formal definition. The informal definition of FOSSIL is that of a person who is locked into old-fashioned and rigid ideas. So, to describe a politician as someone with FOSSILIZED beliefs might suggest that his views would have been appropriate in the Stone Age.

Word Link: REMAINS

Memory Key: After you've sung do, re, mi, FA, SOL (FOSSIL) what REMAINS is la, ti, do.

HYBRID
(HIGH brid)—blended; mixed; composed of different elements

In its strict scientific sense, a HYBRID is any plant or animal that results from the cross-fertilization of two different varieties, races, breeds, or species. The tangelo, for example, is a HYBRID of an orange and a tangerine. And have you ever heard of a beefalo, a HYBRID of a cow and buffalo bred for beef? Most of the time HYBRIDS are intentionally created, but some of my favorite dogs have been unintentional HYBRIDS, that is, mongrels. As far as its nonscientific usage goes, HYBRID can be used in most situations where you want to convey the sense of a blend or mix. In its original form, the game of basketball was conceived of as a HYBRID of several sports, among them soccer, football, and hockey.

Word Link: MIXTURE

Memory Key: Scientists sometimes MIX genes to produce a HIGH BREED (HYBRID) of a particular animal. Think of the process as a HIGH BREED MIX.

CLONE
—to duplicate organisms that are identical from a single common ancestor, such as a cell

CLONING is the process by which organisms are produced from the genetic material of a single individual and not through the normal process of fertilization. Botanists have known about CLONING for decades, but lately there has been a good deal of talk and much controversy about animal and human CLONING. The idea behind CLONING is not only to create a new organism but to <u>duplicate</u> the original one. The subject of CLONING is the theme of a number of novels and a popular movie, <u>The Boys from Brazil,</u> which dealt with the attempts of a group of Nazi officers to produce a CLONE of Adolf Hitler.

<u>Word Link:</u> DUPLICATE

<u>Memory Key:</u> A fragrance processed to smell exactly like another could be called a DUPLICATE COLOGNE (CLONE).

FISSION
(FISH un)—splitting or breaking up into two parts; the splitting of an atomic nucleus, resulting in the release of energy

Certain words are like labels pinned to the pages of time. They tell the story of an age. FISSION is such a word. Its underlying meaning is the spontaneous division of a cell or small organism into new cells and organisms—in other words, a biological term. But then the physicists picked it up to denote the splitting of the nuclei of atoms (nuclear FISSION) into two parts releasing stupendous quantities of energy. It is this release of energy in an atomic bomb that creates the devastating force. A controlled fission reaction takes place in the nuclear reactors in utility plants producing a continuous source of energy for electric power.

Word Link: SPLIT

Memory Key: When you divide a fishing expedition into parts, you get SPLIT FISHIN' (FISSION).

SYNERGISM

(SIN ur jiz'm)—an interaction of two or more separate components of any kind which, when combined, achieve a greater total effect than if they acted alone or when their individual effects are added up

SYNERGISM has a theological origin and was initially used in the eighteenth century to describe the cooperative effort between God's grace and a person's own activity in regeneration—spiritual rebirth. Eventually, scientists plucked the word out of its religious niche and used SYNERGY to explain what happens when certain agents, such as drugs for example, are combined to produce an effect that is greater than the sum of their individual results.

Because of the impact of science on our vocabulary, SYNERGY is a part of our everyday language. Someone might describe a marriage as having a SYNERGISTIC effect on the people involved. This means that the marriage as a unit is greater than the individual qualities or talents of each person.

Word Link: INTERACT

Memory Key: When a popular rock group INTERACTS with fans at an autograph session, the result is a SIGNING ORGY (SYNERGY). Think of SIGNING ORGY INTERACTION.

BINARY ═══════════════════════════════════════
(BY nair ee)—Involving two alternatives. The word is widely used in any situation involving two parts.

BINARY is a word that's much more familiar to computer opera-tors and biologists than to the general public. The reason com-puter operators know it so well is that information is stored in computers in BINARY units, that is, a system using the two sym-bols 0 and 1. The larger the computer, the more BINARY units that can be combined. Biologists, on the other hand, think of the word as involving the separation of cells or organisms into two parts, as in BINARY division. Deal with a printer and you may hear him speak of a BINARY color. That's a color obtained by combining two primary colors, such as yellow and blue producing green. And I know an executive who likes to respond to requests with a BINARY reply. "My answer," he says, "is either yes or no."

Word Link: TWO

Memory Key: A couple of days of breeze means that it's BEEN AIRY (BINARY) for TWO days.

EMPIRICAL ═══════════════════════════════════
(em PIR i k'l)—based on direct or practical experience

EMPIRICAL means "based on practical experience and observa-tion as opposed to theoretical knowledge." An EMPIRICAL idea is one that has already worked for you and others. It's not an idea you've envisioned and never tried. When an advertising company launches a campaign, the copy in the advertisement, the layout, the publications, and spots on TV and radio are all usually based on EMPIRICAL knowledge of what has been successful in the past. The word itself came from doctors in ancient Greece who believed that the practice of medicine should depend on observation and experiments and not on unfounded theories. And this EMPIRICAL method was mostly trial and error. Before you feel too sorry for their patients, remember that your doctor has an EMPIRI-CAL side to him also: "Let's try these pills and see if they work."

Essentially, experiential has the same connotation as EMPIRI-CAL, though it's become something of a vogue word. It's just another way of saying something is based on direct experience. EMPIRICAL is, I think, a richer and more interesting word.

Word Link: EXPERIENCE

Memory Key: You need EXPERIENCE to UMPIRE A COW's (EM-PIRICAL) baseball game.

Word Game

Which of the alternate choices, A or B, is more closely related to the numbered word on the left? Underline your answer.

1. binary	A. two-fold	B. annually
2. synergism	A. interaction	B. destruction
3. fission	A. sound	B. splitting
4. clone	A. duplicate	B. foolish person
5. hybrid	A. pure breed	B. blend
6. fossil	A. old remains	B. recent discovery
7. catalyst	A. destroyer	B. stimulus
8. galaxy	A. planet	B. vast group
9. biodegradable	A. indestructible	B. decomposable
10. empirical	A. direct experience	B. empire building

Answers: 1-A 2-A 3-B 4-A 5-B 6-A 7-B 8-B 9-B 10-A

Word Game II

Fill in the blank with the appropriate word:

1. A person whose presence at a party seems to liven things up is sometimes referred to as a _____.

2. One of the ways you can insult an older person who has stubborn, archaic views is to call that person a _____.

3. If you want to refer to someone whose political views are exactly the same as those of his predecessors, you might describe him as a political _____.

4. Two people who bring out the best in each other represent an example of _____.

5. Ecologists are in favor of packaging products that are _____.

6. The convention drew a _____ of famous people.

7. A nectarine is an example of a _____ fruit.

8. A situation involving two alternatives might be described as _____.

9. A splitting into two parts that releases energy is known as _____.

10. The research was based on an _____ approach.

Answers: 1. catalyst 2. fossil 3. clone 4. synergism 5. biodegrada-ble 6. galaxy 7. hybrid 8. binary 9. fission 10. empirical

Word Game ▯▯▯

Match the word on the left with the word link on the right, and think of the memory key.

1. binary	A. experience
2. synergism	B. stimulus
3. fission	C. split
4. clone	D. mixture
5. hybrid	E. decompose
6. fossil	F. star
7. galaxy	G. remains
8. catalyst	H. duplicate
9. biodegradable	I. interact
10. empirical	J. two

Answers: 1-J 2-I 3-C 4-H 5-D 6-G 7-F 8-B 9-E 10-A

V
Heaven on Earth

WEEK 1, DAY 3

Who knows? Maybe it's your <u>karma</u> to have such a terrible bowling score some night that you become an <u>anathema</u> to your teammates. If that happens, it's time to rely on your <u>mantra</u> and sink into a blissful state of <u>nirvana.</u> Who cares? There's nothing <u>sacrosanct</u> about winning. Anyway, your time out will give you a chance to review the ten words in this section which relate to various religions in the world. As you probably know already, all of them have established a permanent place for themselves in our everyday conversation.

anathema
ecumenical
nirvana
mantra
secular
schism
scruple
karma
sacrosanct
apostasy

ANATHEMA
(uh NATH uh muh)—whatever is detestable or hated

In ancient Greece, the mythological god Zeus had his thunderbolt to hurl at whoever was unfortunate enough to incur his anger. In the Middle Ages the Church had its equivalent of the thunderbolt —the ANATHEMA. This was a curse coupled with excommunication (official separation) from the Church and used against backsliders and sinners. People believed that on dying the luckless soul would go straight to hell. Today in church circles the word has taken on the meaning of "to ban," in the sense of a book, a play, an idea. At one time the Roman Catholic Church pronounced an ANATHEMA against the teachings of Freud.

More commonly we use ANATHEMA to convey the notion of something being detested or hated. Hitler's name, for instance, is still an ANATHEMA to millions of people throughout the world. It's probably stretching a point to say that most children view spinach as an ANATHEMA. Then again, maybe not.

Word Link: HATE

Memory Key: If you don't like to study science, you would probably HATE ANATOMY (ANATHEMA).

ECUMENICAL
(ek you MEN i k'l)—universal; worldwide, specifically relating to worldwide religious unity

There has been a growing movement toward bringing the various branches of the Christian church more closely together to encourage a greater sense of understanding and mutual appreciation. This growing cooperation between Protestants, Roman Catholics, members of the Eastern Orthodox Church, and others is called ECUMENISM. There are currently many ECUMENICAL organizations working together to promote world peace. A New York–based organization called the World Council of Churches has as its goal the ECUMENICAL idea of worldwide Christian unity.

Word Link: WORLDWIDE

Memory Key: There was WORLDWIDE turmoil when the Ayatol-lAH KHOMENI (ECUMENICAL) called for the return of the Shah of Iran.

NIRVANA
(nur VA nuh)—the Buddhist's state of supreme bliss

NIRVANA comes into the English language via Buddha. The word tends to mean different things to different people. You see the word more and more today whenever a writer or speaker wants to convey the idea of supreme happiness, regardless of the situation. NIRVANA to a true gourmet, for instance, might be a two-week tour of the finest restaurants in Paris. Buddha, however, had a far stricter concept of the term. To Buddhists NIRVANA is the state of mind you achieve once you train your mind to overcome the pressures of desire, illusion, hatred, envy, loneliness, and the like. Buddha thought of his teachings as a kind of raft that carried people to safety, peace, happiness, and tranquillity—to a freedom from all worldly cares.

Word Link: BLISS

Memory Key: Think of a NERVE ON A (NIRVANA) portion of the brain that controls happiness, the BLISS NERVE.

MANTRA

(MAN truh)—in Hinduism, a sacred passage used as a prayer

The enormous popularity of MANTRA seems to indicate that many people are searching for an inner peace. The word comes from Sanskrit and meant "an instrument of thought" or "the sound whose effects are known." MANTRA became the "in" word of the 1960s when Maharishi Mahesh Yogi promoted a particular way of meditating called Transcendental Meditation. Each of his followers receives a MANTRA, a short, sacred sound from one of the ancient Hindu scripts. The follower is urged to meditate twice a day, thinking on the MANTRA. The word has been picked up now by people of other faiths. A MANTRA used by some Christians is "my God my all," a prayer of St. Francis of Assisi.

Word Link: PRAYER

Memory Key: When a MAN TRUSTS (MANTRA) PRAYER, it means he has a strong belief in God.

SECULAR

(SEK yuh ler)—worldly; having material rather than spiritual concerns

To describe something as SECULAR is to say, simply, that it has nothing whatsoever to do with religion. SECULAR is a neutral word. It isn't meant to pass judgment one way or the other. Most of the music we listen to, the books we read, and the entertainment we see is SECULAR, that is, nonreligious in nature. And the public school system in the United States is SECULAR education because religion and education are separated by law.

Word Link: NONRELIGIOUS

<u>Memory Key:</u> If an atheist wrote a book filled with stories about bicycles, it might be called NONRELIGIOUS CYCLE LORE (SEC-ULAR).

SCHISM
(SIZ 'm)—a division or separation into groups or sects because of different beliefs or opinions

SCHISM is a troublesome word to pronounce. The correct pro-nunciation is more like <u>scissors,</u> that is, SIZ 'm. The word has a religious origin and was once used exclusively in reference to splits or breaches in the Christian churches, such as the SCHISM in the ninth century between the Greek and Latin churches. These days, however, you can use the word in almost any situation in which one group splits away from another because of a conflict of opinions, such as SCHISMS within political parties.

<u>Word Link:</u> SPLIT

<u>Memory Key:</u> When you're SPLITTING logs, it's always good to SIZE 'M (SCHISM) up, before you swing the ax. First you SIZE 'M up, then you SPLIT.

SCRUPLE
(SCREW p'l)—a doubt as to what is right or fair

If you're a person who frequently questions what you do in terms of its being right or fair, it would be accurate to describe you as somebody with SCRUPLES. If, on the other hand, you rarely have any qualms or misgivings about what you do and seldom consider the ethical implications of your actions, you could be called UN-SCRUPULOUS, someone lacking in SCRUPLES. Agents of the FBI once masqueraded as wealthy Arabs and offered bribes to various members of Congress. One midwestern senator had a SCRUPLE about the request and turned it down. Other congress-men apparently were UNSCRUPULOUS and accepted the bribes. SCRUPLE pertains to a special characteristic—a particular sense of doubt or misgiving—that usually is enough to prevent dishonest actions.

Word Link: QUALM

Memory Key: If somebody asked you to dive into a pool filled with screws, a SCREW POOL, you couldn't be blamed for having QUALMS about it. You would have SCREW POOL (SCRUPLE) QUALMS.

KARMA

(KAR muh)—the destiny of a person as determined by previous acts

KARMA is a Hindu as well as a Buddhist word. The idea behind it is that sooner or later everything we do or think brings its de-served punishment or reward, even if this occurs in a subsequent life. Your KARMA is the blueprint of your present life as previously established by what you've done in a past life. We tend to use KARMA figuratively today as fate or destiny, seeing good KARMA in the life of a person who has been blessed with good fortune and bad KARMA in the life of someone harassed by misfortune. A music magazine referring to a singer wrote that "his recording career has been plagued with an unusually bad KARMA." May your KARMA be all good.

Word Link: DESTINY

Memory Key: A CAR MUST (KARMA) eventually wear out; that is its DESTINY.

SACROSANCT ════════════════

(SAC row sankt)—sacred; holy; inviolable

SACROSANCT began its life as a strictly religious word, used in the description of any place or object imbued with extraordinary holiness. When God says to Moses in Exodus, "Take off your shoes for you are standing on holy ground," he refers to a SACROSANCT spot. Today SACROSANCT has wide application in the secular world. The takeover of the American Embassy by young Iranian militants proved, for instance, that international embassies are no longer as SACROSANCT as people once thought. And in some parts of the world there is growing concern that where human rights were once thought to be inviolable (protected from violation), they are no longer as SACROSANCT as they once were.

Word Link: SACRED

Memory Key: A row of sacks containing SACRED rosaries just sank in a river before your eyes. You were there when the SACRED SACK of ROSaries SANK (SACROSANCT).

APOSTASY ════════════════

(a POS ta see)—defection or rejection of one's faith, party, or principles

Years ago if you were accused of APOSTASY, it meant that you had totally repudiated your religious faith. That is, you defected from what you formerly professed to believe. If you'd been a Roman Catholic you would have been immediately excommunicated. Today, however, the word is used more generally. The writer Arthur Koestler, who had once been a Communist, was branded by the Kremlin as an APOSTATE when he publicly denounced communism. Occasionally a Democrat becomes a Republican and vice versa. If they know the word, party stalwarts would call this jumping of traces an APOSTASY.

It will help you to remember the word if you can break it up into its various parts. For example, the prefix apo means "away" and histemi, "to stand." So an APOSTASY is a standing away from your faith. Apo is found in other words: apogee, the point of the moon's orbit farthest "away" from the earth; apoplexy is a stroke where the power of voluntary motion is taken "away"; the apostles were sent "away" to bear witness of Christ.

Word Link: DEFECTION

Memory Key: When you DEFECT from a group it means you are OPPOSED TO SEEing (APOSTASY) them.

Word Game ⌐

Write true or false next to the following statements:

1. A <u>mantra</u> is a prayer you say only once. _____

2. <u>Nirvana</u> is a state of mind characterized by nervousness. _____

3. Many people consider holy objects <u>sacrosanct.</u> _____

4. Being without <u>scruples</u> means having qualms. _____

5. The best place to look for <u>secular</u> books is inside a church library. _____

6. If you've been plagued by misfortune throughout your life, you might say that your <u>karma</u> is bad. _____

7. Groups that achieve unity form a <u>schism.</u> _____

8. You will usually go out of your way to avoid an <u>anathema.</u> _____

9. A priest with <u>ecumenical</u> interests has no concern for nonchurch matters. _____

10. <u>Apostasy</u> is heresy. _____

Answers: 1-F 2-F 3-T 4-F 5-F 6-T 7-F 8-T 9-F 10-T

Word Game ⅠⅠ

Match the words in the left-hand column with the word in the right-hand column that comes closest in meaning:

1. anathema	A. rejection of belief
2. ecumenical	B. prayer
3. nirvana	C. separation
4. schism	D. not sacred
5. scruple	E. very holy
6. karma	F. destiny
7. sacrosanct	G. universal
8. secular	H. bliss
9. mantra	I. curse
10. apostasy	J. reluctance

Answers: 1-I 2-G 3-H 4-C 5-J 6-F 7-E 8-D 9-B 10-A

Word Game III

Write the word link next to each word. Think of the memory image.

1. secular _____
2. sacrosanct _____
3. karma _____
4. scruple _____
5. schism _____
6. mantra _____
7. nirvana _____
8. ecumenical _____
9. anathema _____
10. apostasy _____

Answers: 1. nonreligious 2. sacred 3. destiny 4. qualm 5. split
6. prayer 7. bliss 8. worldwide 9. hate 10. defection

VI

Weather to Go or Not

Gone are the days when a weather report consisted of a recitation of high and low temperatures for the day. Now that meteorology, the study of weather and climate, has become an established field in its own right, words relating to the subject have assumed a general importance they may have once lacked. Here are ten weather-, atmospheric-, and environment-related words. You've probably heard some of them before, but their precise meanings may surprise you.

solstice
arid
habitat
ecology
precipitate
seismic
miasma
occlude
tectonic
halcyon

SOLSTICE

(SOUL stis)—the longest day (June 22) and the shortest day (December 22)

SOLSTICE is a word used by certain erudite weather people at least twice a year. It refers to either of two days when the sun is at its farthest point south or north of the equator. On one day during the <u>winter</u> SOLSTICE (December 22) the sun is at its farthest point south of the equator, meaning less sun for us living in the Northern Hemisphere. But for such places as Brazil, Australia, and other countries "south of the border" they are getting maximum sunlight and that day is the official start of their summer. The situation is reversed six months later during the day of the <u>summer</u> SOLSTICE (June 22) when the sun is farthest north of the equator (over our heads) while our neighbors in the Southern Hemisphere are buttoning up their overcoats for winter.

<u>Word Link:</u> FAR AWAY

<u>Memory Key:</u> The two musical symbols, SOLS and TIS (SOLSTICE) are FAR AWAY from DO.

ARID

(AR id)—dry; parched; without interest

Picture a desert wasteland where it never rains and where virtually nothing can grow in the soil. The adjective best used to describe such a land is ARID. But as with so many words in the English language, ARID can be used also in the figurative sense. If you want to describe a book or a play in which the ideas expressed are sterile and have no life, ARID is a perfectly acceptable word. But a word of warning: Don't be in too much of a hurry to use ARID interchangeably with the synonym <u>dry.</u> There are <u>dry</u> wines (wines that aren't sweet) but no ARID wines. And a person with a keen sense of wit might be pleased if you described his sense of humor as <u>dry,</u> but might take exception if you described it as ARID. And we complain about the difficulties of other languages!

Word Link: DRY

Memory Key: If you're at the beach, the only way to DRY a wet towel is to AIR IT (ARID).

HABITAT
(HAB i tat)—region where something normally lives or is found

HABITAT sounds like a word you might use as a substitute for house or dwelling, but it's incorrect to use the term within this narrow context. Yes, HABITAT does imply the idea of a <u>home base,</u> though it incorporates not only the <u>place</u> but the conditions of the overall environment. The HABITAT of kangaroos, for instance, is the outback of Australia. Crops such as tobacco and cotton are found only in certain HABITATS where the soil and climate are conducive to their growth. One reason people use this word incorrectly is that they confuse it with <u>habitation,</u> which does in fact refer to a more permanent dwelling. Both of these words, HABITAT and <u>habitation,</u> relate similarly to the adjective <u>habitable,</u> "fit to be lived in."

Word Link: HOME

Memory Key: When you learn a good HABIT AT (HABITAT) HOME, it stays with you wherever you go.

ECOLOGY

(ee KOL oh jee)—the science of the "balance of nature" or the interrelationship of organisms and their environment

ECOLOGY is a powerhouse of a word that challenges the way we all live and think. It encapsulates the concept of a world held together in a delicate and subtle balance, a world in which there is an interrelationship in the total environment of everything that creates and sustains life—earth, atmosphere, sea, all animate as well as inanimate things. When something gets out of ECOLOGICAL balance all hell can break loose, as you might expect. In parts of Africa bad farming and hunting practices have turned fertile land into deserts, dooming hundreds of thousands of people to starvation and thirst. In our own Southwest we had the dust bowl, the result of farmers plowing up the prairies, throwing the environment out of ECOLOGICAL balance. And how are we to counter the devastating ECOLOGICAL effects of acid rain?

Word Link: BALANCE

Memory Key: One way of stressing the BALANCE implied in the term ECOLOGY is to call the science EQUALOGY (ECOLOGY).

PRECIPITATE

(pri SIP uh tate)—To bring on hastily or prematurely; hurl head-long. As an adjective—overhasty; rash; impetuous; also PRECIPI-TOUS.

If you watch television news, you know that precipitation is a weather term referring either to falling rain or snow. This is a logical extension of the Latin praecipitare, "to throw headlong or hurl downward."

The root also gives us the interesting word PRECIPITATE. The central meaning is that of a rash and premature action or thought, or something done impulsively without adequate preparation, which reflects its Latin origin. Politics is always a hotbed of PRE-CIPITATE (or PRECIPITOUS) action and a local newspaper called the township's increase in the property tax PRECIPITATE and unwarranted.

Sometimes people confuse PRECIPITATE and the word <u>cause</u> as synonyms, using them interchangeably. This is incorrect usage. <u>Cause</u> is a broad term describing whatever it is that contributes to an effect. PRECIPITATE has a specific connotation implying a suddenness. For example, a thoughtless statement can PRECIPI-TATE (bring about suddenly) an argument. A thoughtless state-ment also may eventually become the <u>cause</u> of a dispute, but does not necessarily PRECIPITATE it.

<u>Word Link:</u> BRING ON SUDDENLY

<u>Memory Key:</u> PRESS A hot POTATO (PRECIPITATE) thought-lessly and you'll BRING ON SUDDENLY a scream.

SEISMIC
(SIZE mic)—characteristic of an earthquake

SEISMIC is a word generally used to describe the tremors of shocks that result from an earthquake, but it has broad figurative use as well. The Wall Street crash in 1929, for instance, had SEISMIC effects on economic markets throughout the world. An associate with whom I shared a hotel room during a business trip to California snored so loudly I couldn't fall asleep. One night in desperation I kicked his bed strongly with my foot. As he sat up suddenly, I feigned sleep while he stayed awake, and for the first time in several nights I got a good rest. When I awoke, he said, "Listen, Funk, you say you're such a light sleeper. That's a lot of baloney. You slept right through an earthquake. You should have felt the way those damned SEISMIC shocks shook up my bed."

Word Link: EARTHSHAKING

Memory Key: Another way of describing an EARTHSHAKING hamburger might be a colossal-SIZED "MAC" (SEISMIC).

MIASMA ══════════════════════════════════
(my AZ ma)—heavy vapor of fog

Many words are born with specific meanings but later take on a more general and figurative connotation. The earliest meaning of MIASMA, for instance, and one that still appears first in the dictionaries, is a thick, vaporous atmosphere coming from marshes such as in the Florida Everglades. It was thought to be unhealthy and old-timers believed it caused malaria. Today it's not surprising that MIASMA's figurative meaning should suggest something like a pervasive vapor, an unwholesome or corruptive atmosphere, situation, or influence. "In this MIASMA of doubt," an economist wrote recently, "we may fail to see that a historical turning point is really possibly at hand."

Word Link: FOG

Memory Key: MY ASTHMA (MIASMA) acts up in the FOG.

OCCLUDE ══════════════════════════════════
(uh KLUDE)—to block, shut off

Here's your chance to disprove the familiar saying "Everybody talks about the weather but nobody does anything about it." Knowing this word may help you to anticipate the caprices of Mother Nature.

Though OCCLUDE can be applied to almost anything that blocks or shuts off, most of the time you see it used medically or with weather forecasts. Medically it describes a type of heart attack when a thrombus (blood clot) OCCLUDES an artery. For your favorite TV weatherman, an OCCLUDED front means that cold air is overtaking a warm front, digging under and blocking or shutting off contact with the earth. Stormy weather is the almost certain result.

Word Link: BLOCK (shut off, cut off)

Memory Key: Think of A CLOUD (OCCLUDE) BLOCKing out the sun.

TECTONIC
(tek TON ick)—pertaining to the earth's crust and the various forces affecting it

TECTONIC can be used in two ways, depending on whether you're talking to an architect or a geologist. If it's the former, your architect friend will employ the word in reference to various aspects of construction, such as design, stress, and other related areas. He may talk to you about the TECTONIC problems of the house. If your friend is a geologist, TECTONIC is a word relating to the actual structure of the earth's crust and the general changes affecting it. If you live over a geological fault, a fracture in the underlying rock structure, and if one or both of the two sides of the fault shift, grating against each other, shock waves radiate out of the surrounding area, causing a TECTONIC earthquake. The other type of earthquake is created by underground volcanic activity.

Word Link: A CRUST

Memory Key: You TAKE TONIC (TECTONIC) to end A CRUSTy feeling in your stomach.

HALCYON

(HAL see un)—HALCYON days are calm and idyllic.

HALCYON days are peaceful and calm, when the skies are clear and the winds still. A HALCYON day has a kind of magic that pulls you outside—for a walk, to lie in the sun, play a sport, or to simply soak in nature's beauty. But use the word also to talk about those happy days in the past you'll never forget, days surrounded by a golden aura. We've all had days on a vacation when everything clicked. They were HALCYON days. If you're a historian, you can discuss the HALCYON days of a particular peaceful and prosperous era in history.

HALCYON days had an actual place on the ancient calendar. They were the fourteen days about the time of the winter solstice. It was during this period that the HALCYON, or kingfisher, was supposed to sit on her nest as it floated in the sea. She was believed to have a magic power to calm the winds and waves so that her nest would be secure.

Word Link: CALM

Memory Key: A fisherman named HAL SEES ON (HALCYON) a clear day fish jumping out of the CALM water.

Word Game

Choose the correct answer from the multiple-choice answers below each phrase:

1. Solstice refers to
    A. heat
    B. time
    C. certain days of the year

2. An arid environment lacks
    A. sun
    B. rain
    C. wind

3. A weather report calling for precipitation means you should carry your
    A. raincoat
    B. sunglasses
    C. overcoat

4. The term seismic refers mainly to
    A. tornadoes
    B. hurricanes
    C. earthquakes

5. You're likely to encounter a miasma in a
    A. swamp area
    B. desert
    C. cold climate

6. Habitat refers to
    A. an animal's habits
    B. where the animal lives
    C. what the animal eats

7. A word closely associated with <u>ecology</u> is
   A. balance
   B. rain
   C. warmth

8. An <u>occluded</u> weather front moving in will bring
   A. pleasant weather
   B. extremely hot temperatures
   C. a storm

9. A <u>tectonic</u> study of an earthquake might show how
   A. the populace reacted
   B. many buildings were damaged
   C. general changes affected the structure of the earth's crust

10. A <u>halcyon</u> day is one on which you can expect
    A. a cyclone
    B. a changing weather cycle
    C. idyllic calm

Answers: 1-C 2-B 3-A 4-C 5-A 6-B 7-A 8-C 9-C 10-C

Word Game ⅠⅠ

Match the words in the left-hand column with their synonyms in the right-hand column:

1. miasma
2. precipitate
3. seismic
4. arid
5. solstice
6. ecology
7. habitat
8. occlude
9. halcyon
10. tectonic

A. longest day
B. fog
C. bring on suddenly
D. science of nature's balance
E. earthshaking
F. dry
G. living place
H. earth's crust
I. to shut off
J. idyllic calm

Answers: 1-B 2-C 3-E 4-F 5-A 6-D 7-G 8-I 9-J 10-H

Word Game III

Write the proper word next to its word link and think of the memory key.

1. home _____
2. dry _____
3. far away _____
4. balance _____
5. bring on suddenly _____
6. fog _____
7. earthshaking _____
8. calm _____
9. a crust _____
10. block _____

Answers: 1. habitat 2. arid 3. solstice 4. ecology 5. precipitate 6. miasma 7. seismic 8. halcyon 9. tectonic 10. occlude

VII

Personally Speaking

How to make your name immortal? Do something to get it in the dictionary. For example, Epicurus was a Greek philosopher who had a special slant on living. Niccolo Machiavelli was an idea man for the politicians of the sixteenth century, and Rabelais a French writer with a gargantuan appetite for life. Such words are known as <u>eponyms,</u> names derived from the name of a real or mythical person. That's the focus of this particular chapter.

protean
epicure
saturnine
nemesis
philistine
Rabelaisian
Machiavellian
pander
Pyrrhic victory
malapropism

You don't have to search in the distant past for illustrations. Charles Boycott lent his name unwillingly to a word we see frequently in the news, while Nicolas Chauvin, a soldier in Napoleon's army, gave birth to a word that's become almost jargon among certain groups of people (chauvinism). Jean Nicot, French ambassador to Portugal, planted some tobacco seeds and millions have been inhaling nicotine ever since. But while you wait for a Funk & Wagnalls or a Webster to discover you, why not use some of the following names in your conversation or writing today?

PROTEAN
(PRO tee un)—changeable; different forms

The essence of PROTEAN is an ability to assume many different forms without losing the basic identity. The changes, in other words, are outer manifestations, the inner being remaining more or less constant. Most of the time we use this word to describe someone blessed with versatile talents. Michelangelo's PROTEAN imagination showed up in his painting, his sculpture and architecture, in his designs and poetry. A woman who finds herself in the role of a wife and mother at the same time tends to develop PROTEAN capabilities as a psychologist, short order cook, paramedic, chauffeur, consultant, playmate, secretary, travel planner, storyteller. You name it. By the way, PROTEAN comes from Proteus, the Roman god of the sea. Since the sea is always changing it is easy to see how the myth grew up that Proteus was capable of assuming any shape he chose.

Word Link: CHANGE

Memory Key: If you go to a store and pay for something in PROTEINS (PROTEAN) you're likely to receive PROTEIN CHANGE.

EPICURE
(EP i cure)—someone who enjoys good and often unusual food and drink

If you love good food and fine wine, you can call yourself a gourmet. But if, in addition to this, you are fastidious in your choices and know just exactly what to order in a restaurant or buy in a store, you can call yourself an EPICURE. EPICURE is a word derived from the name of the Greek philosopher Epicurus, who believed that pleasure was the highest good but who also taught his followers to do all things in moderation in order to prevent the consequences of overindulgence. EPICURE, then, conveys not only the idea of pleasure but the idea of discrimination as well. It is used more loosely today so you can take EPICUREAN delight in almost anything—painting, architecture, books, gardens, even automobiles.

Word Link: PLEASURE

Memory Key: It's possible to draw a great deal of PLEASURE from A PICTURE (EPICURE).

SATURNINE ═══════════════════════════════
(SAT ur nine)—having a serious, gloomy, and often forbidding disposition

A gloomy and morose person usually wears a SATURNINE expression. Yet the origin of this word doesn't suggest anything gloomy at all. SATURNINE comes from the Roman god Saturn, who took care of agriculture and was, for this reason, the god of happiness and plenty and of the golden and Saturnian days. Somehow, though, this divinity lent his name to the planet Saturn, the sixth planet in distance from the sun. And since Saturn was so remote, people thought of it as chilly and gloomy. These are the qualities now attributed to SATURNINE people who may have a SATURNINE disposition or outlook. The word is more at home in literary discussions than in everyday conversation.

Word Link: GLOOMY

Memory Key: Visualize two 9's. The one on the left is GLOOMIER than the one on the right. It's a SADDER NINE (SATURNINE).

NEMESIS

(NEM uh sis)—retribution; vengeance; something destructive or ruinous

NEMESIS is a powerful word that can be used also in a light-hearted way. "Chocolate cake is my NEMESIS," a person might say. "I can't resist it." On one level, a NEMESIS refers to whatever frustrates or blocks you or even what destroys you. On another it is when you get the swift kick in the pants you deserve. Inflation is the NEMESIS of the latter part of the twentieth century, largely the result of our indulgences, and is retribution. Knowing where the word comes from may help you to remember it. Among the active Greek Gods was Nemesis, the goddess of retribution and of righteous anger. She punished pretentiousness and crimes with her sword and her lethal, swift avenging wings. It didn't pay to cross her.

Word Link: ENEMY

Memory Key: If you are a member of a feuding family, someone might ask you to NAME A SISTER (NEMESIS) you consider an ENEMY.

PHILISTINE

(FIL is teen)—narrow-minded, prosaic person; someone antago-nistic to art and culture

If you know your Bible, you know the Philistines were an unenlight-ened, warlike people who were constantly harassing the Israelites until Samson put an end to their dominance. The Philistines were never again a force to be reckoned with in Palestine, but the word PHILISTINE lives on. We use it to describe people who are driven mainly by materialistic values and disinterested in intellectual, spiritual, and artistic matters. The writer James T. Farrell once described a PHILISTINE as a person who likes to talk about morals but doesn't understand what is morally wrong. I like to think that the mere fact of your reading this book means that you are definitely <u>not</u> a PHILISTINE.

<u>Word Link:</u> ANTI-INTELLECTUAL

<u>Memory Key:</u> An <u>ANTI-INTELLECTUAL</u> FILLS HIS TIME (PHILISTINE) with materialistic activities.

RABELAISIAN
(rab uh LAY zhun)—coarsely humorous; boisterous

Some people make such an indelible mark upon their time that their name becomes part of the language. Take François Rabelais, the sixteenth-century French scholar, humanist, physician, and satirist. Rabelais was known primarily for his robust humor, his biting satires of politics, education, and religion, and for his celebration of the natural life. So to describe any person or any work as being RABELAISIAN is to credit it with these very qualities. I have a good friend whose RABELAISIAN sense of humor is a little too coarse for some people I know, but he's a wonderful companion to have around at a dull party.

<u>Word Link:</u> EARTHY

<u>Memory Key:</u> A museum specimen of EARTHY material from an Asian city might be titled, RUBBLE, ASIAN (RABELAISIAN).

MACHIAVELLIAN

(mac ee uh VEL ee un)—crafty; treacherous; characterizing duplicity

Judging from the synonyms for MACHIAVELLIAN—unscrupulous, unprincipled, expedient, opportunistic, conniving, calculating, deceitful, self-serving—you would think that the man whose name inspired this word was one of the great villians of history. Actually, however, Niccolo Machiavelli, the Italian statesman and author, was a model citizen and a loving family man and his works, especially his masterpiece, The Prince, are not as completely immoral as some people think. Machiavelli did maintain that rulers are justified in the use of deception and unfortunately, on occasion, treachery in order to hold onto their arbitrary powers. His theories, however, were mainly a reflection of his pessimism about the human condition and his wish for a good and just society. All the same, the word today is used to describe people who are crafty and cunning enough to manipulate others and events to their own advantage.

Word Link: MANIPULATE

Memory Key: In order to MAKE A VEIL (MACHIAVELLIAN) you have to MANIPULATE a needle and thread.

PANDER

(PANder)—to cater to or exploit the weaknesses or worst desires in others

PANDER reveals the worst in human nature. The basic meaning is to act as a pimp or a go-between in illicit love affairs, but the word has taken on the broader meaning of catering to the lower tastes and desires of people and exploiting their weaknesses. So many books, films, and TV programs promote kinky sex, unnecessary violence, sadism, and the like, PANDERING to a gullible and vulnerable public. However, the word also has a somewhat less pejorative emphasis, suggesting a catering to self-serving concerns. For instance, sometimes politicians PANDER to special interest groups, ignoring a responsibility to the nation as a whole.

PANDER wasn't always a negative word. In Greek mythology Pandarus was a respectable Greek hero in the Trojan War. But the English poet Chaucer and Shakespeare in his play <u>Troilus and Cressida</u> represented Pandarus as a pimp who found the girl Cressida for Troilus, the king of Troy.

<u>Word Link:</u> CATER (exploit)

<u>Memory Key:</u> The CATERER said, "Give me the PAN, DEAR (PANDER)."

PYRRHIC VICTORY
(PEER ick)—a victory won at too great a cost

To win a PYRRHIC VICTORY is to win the battle but at a cost so high you may have lost the whole war. Now and then an employee will exaggerate the importance of a point of contention between him and his boss. The incident becomes blown out of proportion and there's a showdown. The employee may prove his point, but meanwhile only wins a PYRRHIC VICTORY, as he hurts his chances for promotion in the company. People who quibble continually over details usually win PYRRHIC VICTORIES at the cost of alienating friends and others.

The word's history is a graphic illustration of how an important word gets created. Pyrrhus was a famous Carthaginian general in the third century B.C. He fought against the Roman army at Asculum where his victory was won at tragic cost, with the finest soldiers of his army being destroyed. After the battle he is supposed to have said, "One more such victory and we are lost." His prediction came true. Thus PYRRHIC VICTORY is one in which the losses are so great that it is no victory at all.

Word Link: VICTORY AT GREAT COST

Memory Key: During a fishing competition from a PIER IT (PYRRHIC) happens you hook Jaws who pulls you in the water and swallows you—A VICTORY AT GREAT COST.

MALAPROPISM
(MAL uh prop is'm)—a humorous misuse of words

MALAPROPISM comes to us from an endearing character, Mrs. Malaprop (from a French phrase, mal à propos, meaning "inopportune"), in The Rivals, a well-known comedy written in 1775 by Richard Sheridan. Mrs. Malaprop could never quite get her tongue to say things properly. She spoke of "an allegory on the banks of the Nile" (instead of alligator) and of her daughter as "a progeny of learning." Her progeny, of course, meant to mean prodigy!

Nearly everybody commits a MALAPROPISM now and then, especially young children. One of my own children used to refer to a successful man we know as a business typhoon. And you can't hear any of Archie Bunker's speeches without detecting a MALAPROPISM every other minute or so. One I remember is, when the family mentioned the Pope's new encyclical, he said, "I don't care if the Pope has taken up bicycling!"

Word Link: MISUSE

Memory Key: To MAIL A PROPELLER IS (MALAPROPISM) to MISUSE the post office.

Word Game

Write true or false next to the following statements:

1. A <u>philistine</u> is usually a well-read person.   _____

2. <u>Saturnine</u> people are good company.   _____

3. <u>Epicureans</u> usually take pleasure in their pursuits.   _____

4. <u>Machiavellian</u> people are not to be trusted too far in business situations.   _____

5. A <u>nemesis</u> is a person whose company you frequently seek out.   _____

6. <u>Protean</u> people are usually one-sided.   _____

7. Quiet, shy people can usually be described as <u>Rabelaisian.</u>   _____

8. TV sometimes will <u>pander</u> to the public's worst instincts.   _____

9. It was a <u>Pyrrhic victory,</u> as he won the argument but lost a friendship.   _____

10. A <u>malapropism</u> brings many laughs.   _____

Answers: 1-F 2-F 3-T 4-T 5-F 6-F 7-F 8-T 9-T 10-T

Word Game II

Fill in the blanks in the following sentences:

1. She takes great pleasure in food and wine; she is an
   _____.

2. His job calls for a multitude of skills and he brings to it
   _____ talents.

3. His _____ skills enable him to manipulate people
   very effectively.

4. The play's coarse humor gave it a _____ flavor.

5. He has bothered me nearly all of my life. He is my
   _____.

6. He has no interest whatsoever in art—he is a true
   _____.

7. The grayness gave the day a _____ feeling.

8. He held to his ideals refusing to _____ to the
   audience.

9. His _____ caused him great embarrassment.

10. He achieved a _____, buying the company of his
    dreams that eventually led to bankruptcy.

Answers: 1. epicure 2. protean 3. Machiavellian 4. Rabelaisian
    5. nemesis 6. philistine 7. saturnine 8. pander 9. malapropism
    10. Pyrrhic victory

Word Game ▯▯▯

Write the proper word next to its memory word link. There are many pictures in these words.

1. enemy _____
2. manipulate _____
3. pleasure _____
4. change _____
5. earthy _____
6. gloomy _____
7. anti-intellectual _____
8. cater _____
9. victory at great cost _____
10. misuse _____

Answers: 1. nemesis 2. Machiavellian 3. epicure 4. protean 5. Rabelaisian 6. saturnine 7. philistine 8. pander 9. Pyrrhic victory 10. malapropism

TEST I

Let's see how well you remember this group of interesting words. A test such as this helps to reinforce them in your memory. Select the definition you believe is the correct answer. Turn to the end of the test to check your results.

1. badger A. beat B. exhaust C. harass
2. galaxy A. vanity B. a vast cluster of stars C. planetary relationships
3. flaunt A. scoff or jeer B. unfold C. show off
4. inundate A. flood B. waver C. specify
5. fossil A. ancient crockery B. architectural dig C. preserved remains of living matter
6. schism A. division or separation B. reverberating sound C. joining together
7. clone A. glue B. duplicate C. manipulate
8. ecumenical A. universal B. friendly C. learned
9. arid A. bad-smelling B. oppressively hot C. dry
10. protean A. nutritious B. changeable C. deceitful
11. karma A. honor B. unending story C. destiny
12. seismic pertaining to: A. an earthquake B. the cosmos C. a startling occurrence

13. Rabelaisian A. coarsely humorous B. rough and ready C. riotous
14. malign A. disorient B. threaten C. slander
15. biodegradable A. polluting B. able to decompose C. shameful
16. cavil A. ridicule B. dissemble C. find fault with
17. subvert A. overthrow B. dig down C. sink
18. hybrid A. carefully selected B. hardy C. blended
19. scruple A. authority B. doubt as to right or wrong C. reaction
20. binary A. multiplex B. essential C. two alternatives
21. mantra A. type of prayer B. cloak C. sea denizen
22. solstice A. worry B. farthest point C. sympathy
23. nemesis A. retribution B. accomplice C. imitator
24. habitat A. appearance B. region where something normally lives C. dress
25. saturnine A. gloomy B. dark C. monstrous
26. ecology A. study of words B. science of causes C. science of balance of nature
27. rescind A. revoke B. admit error C. apologize and make amends
28. catalyst A. calamity B. condition of muscular rigidity C. stimulus
29. synergism pertaining to: A. a composing of opposites B. a working together C. balance
30. precipitate A. bring on suddenly B. obscurity C. weakness
31. epicure a person who is: A. temperate B. discriminating C. sarcastic
32. philistine A. materialist B. close-fitting garment C. wrestler's belt
33. miasma A. mirage B. vapor C. bog
34. wreak A. twist B. soak C. inflict
35. substantiate A. indicate B. confirm C. emphasize
36. nirvana A. hopelessness B. nervous state C. supreme bliss
37. burgeon A. cover B. force C. grow
38. anathema A. something detested B. unreasoning anger C. compelling necessity

39. fission A. crevasse B. union by melting C. division by splitting
40. secular A. ensuing B. erotic C. worldly
41. Machiavellian A. mechanical B. crafty C. assassinating by poison
42. sacrosanct A. everyday B. peaceful C. sacred
43. empirical based on A. experience B. theory C. power
44. tectonic pertaining to: A. prehistoric era B. earth's crust C. precision
45. pander A. to cater to other's weaknesses B. implore C. take unlawfully
46. malapropism A. misuse of words B. cliché C. harmful activity
47. occlude A. complete B. reflect C. block
48. Pyrrhic victory—victory gained by: A. ruinous loss B. a few over many C. overwhelming
49. apostasy A. desertion of faith B. vision C. missionary zeal
50. halcyon A. stirred up B. calm C. shimmering

Answers: 1-C 2-B 3-C 4-A 5-C 6-A 7-B 8-A 9-C 10-B 11-C 12-A 13-A 14-C 15-B 16-C 17-A 18-C 19-B 20-C 21-A 22-B 23-A 24-B 25-A 26-C 27-A 28-C 29-B 30-A 31-B 32-A 33-B 34-C 35-B 36-C 37-C 38-A 39-C 40-C 41-B 42-C 43-A 44-B 45-A 46-A 47-C 48-A 49-A 50-B

Undoubtedly some of these words are stumbling blocks for you: It's hard for you to remember them. To lock them more securely in your memory, write the words on a three- by five-inch card and look at them for a few moments each day. And then use them!

VIII
International Flavors

WEEK 2, DAY 1

"Neither a borrower nor a lender be," advises a character in Shakespeare's play <u>Hamlet.</u> But our English language flouts this advice. Borrow! It doesn't borrow. It <u>steals</u> words from other languages. It takes them <u>carte blanche.</u> This chapter is a good example. People won't think you're <u>quixotic</u> if you have as your <u>cachet</u> a well-supplied vocabulary which includes foreign words. In fact, your <u>status quo</u> will rise and you won't have to <u>kowtow</u> to anyone linguistically. Adopt a workable <u>modus operandi</u> to learn a few new words a day. It's the <u>sine qua non</u> of an inquiring mind. And now on to the next page to continue with your linguistic pilfering.

quixotic
cachet
carte blanche
<u>modus operandi</u>
status quo
incommunicado
graffiti
kowtow
sine qua non
contretemps

QUIXOTIC

(kwik SOT ik)—being idealistic in an utterly impractical way; having noble, romantic ideas that have no chance of success

QUIXOTIC is one of many colorful words that we've inherited directly from literature, in this case from the character Don Quixote (kee OH tee), in the famous novel by the Spanish writer Miguel de Cervantes. The novel is a satire on the silly books of romantic chivalry that were popular during the early part of the seventeenth century, and Don Quixote, who mistakes windmills for giants and prostitutes for virgin maidens, is the embodiment of romantic idealism. Yet, foolish though he may have been as a person, Don Quixote's ideals were high and his motives pure. He was against the falseness and hypocrisy of his time, and was an ardent spokesman for truth and kindness. This is why to be called QUIXOTIC is not so bad, for sometimes a QUIXOTIC personality can stimulate us to a finer vision of life.

Word Link: UNREALISTIC

Memory Key: If you think you can use the QUICK of your thumbnail as a SAW (QUIXOTIC) to cut wood, you're being UNREALISTIC, to say the least.

CACHET

(ka SHAY)—prestige, status

Gucci loafers. Rolex watches. A Rolls-Royce. These are just a few of the expensive status symbols in our society that confer a sense of CACHET, "prestige or status" upon the person who owns them. CACHET is something many people work very hard at getting, and, in some circles, it's more important than money. An actor I know once rationalized his low-paying but prestigious role in a play by saying, "I'd rather have the CACHET than the cash."

Word Link: PRESTIGE

Memory Key: If you can CASH A (CACHET) check in the best restaurants, you obviously have a good deal of PRESTIGE.

CARTE BLANCHE
(cart BLAHNSH)—unlimited authority; full discretionary power; having a free hand

In France, a CARTE BLANCHE is simply a white or blank card. But the French use the term to describe any document that is signed though left blank, allowing you to fill it in as you please. The term has even broader application in English, where it refers to any situation in which you have the authority to do anything you want or spend as much as you want. I have a friend who enjoys just such authority for the large game company he works for. He has CARTE BLANCHE discretion in the creation and designing of all the electronic games. And he isn't even French.

Word Link: FREE REIN

Memory Key: You can give FREE REIN to the horse that draws a CART named BLANCHE (CARTE BLANCHE) and he'll take you anywhere you want to go.

MODUS OPERANDI
(mo dus ahp uh RAN dee)—a procedure; a systematic way of working

Many of the things we do in our everyday lives are based around some sort of planning, but this doesn't mean we have a MODUS OPERANDI for everything we do. This Latin phrase implies the idea of a very systematic, very deliberate approach. My wife, for instance, is a much better shopper than I am. Her MODUS OPE-RANDI takes her efficiently from one store to another without any backtracking, while too often my shopping lacks a MODUS OPE-RANDI and is incurably haphazard.

Word Link: SYSTEM

Memory Key: Give me a MODEST SUPPER AND I (MODUS OPE-RANDI) can plan a SYSTEM to cook it.

STATUS QUO
(STAY tus kwo)—the existing situation or state of affairs

STATUS QUO is one of the roughly 60 percent of English words based on Latin and one of a smaller but still substantial number of words that continues to live on in English in its Latin form. You use the phrase in any number of different situations when you want to convey the notion of "as is." Alert international bankers are interested in the STATUS QUO (existing situation) of the world's economic conditions.

Don't get tripped up by the word status. Some people confuse it with STATUS QUO. Status has to do with relationships between people or things. For example, what is the status of your doctor among his peers? How does he rate? New York City's status as a tourist attraction is tops. Status also implies feelings about prestige and social position.

Word Link: EXISTING STATE

Memory Key: A doctor's statement about the EXISTING STATE of a patient could be called a STATUS QUOTE (STATUS QUO).

INCOMMUNICADO

(in kuh mu nuh KAH do)—without means of communication with other people or the outside world; in solitary confinement

INCOMMUNICADO has a crisp staccato sound similar to the Spanish dance, the flamenco. And it is also another example of how English has borrowed from almost every language in the world. We've taken this word directly from Spanish without so much as changing the spelling. To be INCOMMUNICADO is to be cut off from communication with the rest of the world. Such a state can either be self-induced or imposed by outside forces.

Word Link: CUT OFF

Memory Key: A German businessman chooses to CUT OFF all information about his INCOME in MUNICH (INCOMMUNICADO).

GRAFFITI

(gra FEE tee)—any scribbling or drawing on walls, doors, and the like

GRAFFITI is the plural form of GRAFFITO, a word we've inherited from the Italian graffio, "to scratch." Normally we associate GRAFFITI with the earthy sayings and scrawlings so obvious on public washroom walls, on telephone booths, on trains, buses, and subways. A statement doesn't have to be obscene to qualify as GRAFFITI. For it isn't so much what is written that makes a message GRAFFITI, it's how and where it's written. "Jesus Saves" is a religious message but one which becomes GRAFFITI wherever we find it painted in large letters where it wasn't originally intended to be. And one of the most widespread examples of GRAFFITI is the ubiquitous "Kilroy Was Here." During World War II it appeared on everything from Hitler's bunker to underwater wrecks.

Word Link: SCRIBBLED

Memory Key: Picture two large GIRAFFE FEET (GRAFFITI) SCRIBBLED on a wall.

KOWTOW ═══════════════════════════════════

(COW tow)—to fawn; to defer in a flattering and servile way; to toady

None of us enjoys KOWTOWING to anybody. Yet in the Far East a KOWTOW is a gesture of respect and as routine as shaking hands is in the Western world. The reason for this difference is that when the English colonized China in the nineteenth century and adopted the word, it lost its polite and reverential aura. The English, you see, considered it unthinkable that they, the elite of the world, should KOWTOW to anybody.

Word Link: BEND OVER

Memory Key: The only way to get a good look at a COW TOE (KOWTOW) is to BEND OVER.

SINE QUA NON ═══════════════════════════════

(SI na kwah NON)—an indispensable requirement; an essential condition.

SINE QUA NON is one of the favorite phrases of the famous writer James Michener, who uses it frequently in conversation and in his thinking. "The term summarizes the search an educated man makes for the essence of things," explains Michener. "You could say that I've spent my life looking for the SINE QUA NON of human existence, the essential core of the matter." You don't have to be James Michener to use this useful Latin phrase. SINE QUA NON means, literally, "without which nothing." Use it whenever you want to describe any quality, property, or idea without whose essence there would be nothing. As Michener advises, "Anytime you want to cut away the verbiage, fumigate the smoke screens, and get down to the heart of the matter, ask yourself, 'What's this guy's SINE QUA NON?' and you'll know how to proceed."

Word Link: ESSENCE

Memory Key: In looking for the ESSENCE of a surrealistic painting, you make out the shape of a nun in an aqua-colored habit. In other words, you SEE AN AQUA NUN (SINE QUA NON).

CONTRETEMPS
(KON truh tahn)—mishap, blunder

CONTRETEMPS is a French word which means an awkward or embarrassing mistake or blunder. Its literal translation is "against the time," contre, "against" and temps, "time"—in other words, a mishap occurring at the worst possible moment. Charlie Chaplin's films are filled with humorous CONTRETEMPS—suspenders breaking which drop the comedian's baggy trousers, or when he wanders into an intimate love scene, or gives someone an inappropriate present.

Another French word similar in meaning to CONTRETEMPS is faux pas, translated as a "false step." It points up the accidental quality to a mistake. Most often the word refers to a social blunder such as a tactless remark or a slip of the tongue. You commit a faux pas when someone asks you to keep a secret and you unexpectedly blurt it out in public.

Word Link: MISHAP

Memory Key: The carpenter created a MISHAP when he measured the COUNTER TOP (CONTRETEMPS) to be six inches high.

Word Game ⬚

Match each word in the left-hand column with the correct meaning in the right-hand column.

1. sine qua non	A. impractical
2. kowtow	B. bow down to
3. graffiti	C. scribbling on walls
4. incommunicado	D. unlimited authority
5. status quo	E. situation as is
6. <u>modus operandi</u>	F. prestige
7. carte blanche	G. essential
8. cachet	H. cut off
9. quixotic	I. way of working
10. contretemps	J. blunder

Answers: 1-G 2-B 3-C 4-H 5-E 6-I 7-D 8-F 9-A 10-J

Word Game ▢▢

Write true or false next to the following statements:

1. Rapid changes contribute to a <u>status quo.</u> _____

2. Fine jewelry carries with it a certain <u>cachet.</u> _____

3. A proud person is eager to <u>kowtow</u> to some-
    body else. _____

4. Prisoners are sometimes held <u>incommunicado.</u> _____

5. A <u>sine qua non</u> of a good marriage is mutual
    respect. _____

6. If you want to limit someone's authority, you
    give them <u>carte blanche.</u> _____

7. If you know something about a person's <u>modus
    operandi,</u> you can usually discover something
    about his personality. _____

8. The only place you can see <u>graffiti</u> is in a mu-
    seum. _____

9. The cabinet members were wary of their lead-
    ers' <u>quixotic</u> tendencies. _____

10. A <u>contretemps</u> is a dynamic new dance step. _____

Answers: 1-F 2-T 3-F 4-T 5-T 6-F 7-T 8-F 9-T 10-F

Word Game ☐☐☐

Write the correct word next to its memory word link.

1. mishap _____
2. scribble _____
3. free rein _____
4. bend over _____
5. existing state _____
6. prestige _____
7. essence _____
8. cut off _____
9. system _____
10. unrealistic _____

Answers: 1. contretemps 2. graffiti 3. carte blanche 4. kowtow
5. status quo 6. cachet 7. sine qua non 8. incommunicado
9. <u>modus operandi</u> 10. quixotic

IX

Legal Eagles

While reading a contract, I noticed a statement in small print that "no representation is made that this form of contract for the sale and purchase of real estate complies with section 5-702 of the General Obligations Law ('Plain English')." Why the devil do we have to legislate "plain English?" Communication is understanding and being understood. Using plain English is just plain common sense. Meanwhile, so that you can fly along and keep up with the legal eagles, here are ten words you will want to learn for your own self-defense.

indict
stipulate
surrogate
inquest
larceny
mitigate
ambiguous
allege
plausible
codicil

INDICT

(in DITE)—to charge with a crime; to accuse of wrongdoing

INDICT is a word best reserved for those situations in which you are doing more than merely criticizing another person but delivering a very serious accusation. In law terminology, an INDICTMENT is a formal and legal accusation which, once made, means the accused person is going to have to defend himself in a law court. But you can use the word in general situations as well. Should you become aware of an activity of an individual or group that is harmful to others, you might want to INDICT the wrongdoing by "speaking out" publicly. There may be nothing official or legal about the accusation, but it does expose the fault. On the other hand, INDICT is too strong a word for minor faults. What husband would dare say to his wife, "I INDICT you of being overweight"?

Word Link: ACCUSE

Memory Key: INDICT gestion (indigestion) is something you might get if you were ACCUSED of a crime.

STIPULATE

(STIP you late)—to specify as a particular condition or requirement of an agreement; to set forth, require

To STIPULATE is to set forth very clearly and precisely, in print or in conversation, what you expect in a contract or in some course of action. The word has a somewhat official aura, but it's perfectly acceptable to use the word in everyday conversation. I can STIPULATE that my teen-age sons get my car home on time. Whether they do or not is something else.

Word Link: SPECIFY

Memory Key: Somebody has asked you to name the dance step you enjoy the least, that is, to SPECIFY the STEP YOU HATE (STIPULATE).

SURROGATE

(SUR uh gate)—substitute; a person having the authority to act in place of another

In legal terminology, a SURROGATE is a person appointed by an authority to act in place of somebody else. But the word has wide application outside legal circles as well. Use it anytime you want to convey the idea of a substitution taking place. A child who has been orphaned or abandoned at an early age is frequently raised by grandparents who take on the role of SURROGATE parents.

Word Link: SUBSTITUTE

Memory Key: Imagine an English lord named SIR O'GATE (SUR-ROGATE), who frequently serves as a SUBSTITUTE guest for the royal family at special functions.

INQUEST

(IN quest)—legal investigation

Some words begin their careers by describing a specific quality or trait but escape these narrow boundaries as they become the overused jargon of experts. INQUEST is a word that has gone in the opposite direction. Originally, the word referred to any legal inquiry by a jury to investigate the facts connected with a civil or criminal case. Today the call for an INQUEST usually indicates that there has been a suspicious death.

Word Link: DEATH INVESTIGATION

Memory Key: IN his QUEST to solve the case, a prosecutor will conduct a DEATH INVESTIGATION, an INQUEST.

LARCENY

(LAR suh nee)—taking things unlawfully

There are a number of words that deal with theft, among them robber, burglar, mugging, and LARCENY. Robbery suggests a face-to-face encounter between the robber and victim. Burglary indicates breaking into a house, apartment building, and the like with the intent to steal. Mugging is a frightening robbery by violence when a victim is attacked.

LARCENY, on the other hand, has a broader meaning and is the legal term for theft. It means simply that someone is trying to take unlawfully whatever belongs to someone else, regardless of the situation. The term includes the attempt to steal, successful or not. There are two kinds of LARCENY: Petty LARCENY usually involves thefts of small amounts, while grand LARCENY is the term applied to larger, more impressive sums. A messenger for an investment house who stole some bonds found himself charged with grand LARCENY.

Word Link: THEFT

Memory Key: A Norwegian named LARS has made a THEFT of a C-note (LARCENY).

MITIGATE

(MIT uh gate)—to moderate; make less severe, harsh, or painful

A dental patient is furious because her appointment has been canceled but she hasn't been informed of it. The receptionist tries to soothe the anger with a profuse apology. In other words, she tries to MITIGATE the anger. The receptionist is successful but the incident leaves her with a headache, so she takes an aspirin, which somewhat MITIGATES her pain.

MITIGATE is one of a cluster of words that carries the notion of easing the pain of or lessening the impact of pain. It is used sometimes interchangeably and incorrectly with two other words, assuage and alleviate. Each of these verbs has its own niche. When you assuage someone's anger, you do it by introducing something pleasant, as the receptionist above might have done by offering to reduce the fee on the next visit. Alleviate, on the other hand, is the word to use when you want to convey the idea of temporary relief, as a sedative given to alleviate the aftereffects of having a tooth pulled. All three words—MITIGATE, assuage, and alleviate—imply the idea of relief, but a knowledgeable wordsmith knows how to relieve the right situation with the right word.

Word Link: LESSEN

Memory Key: If you were to OMIT A GATE (MITIGATE) from the design of a garden, you could LESSEN the number of entrances.

AMBIGUOUS ─────────────────────────────
(am BIG you us)—not clear, equivocal, imprecise, vague, indefinite

Years ago, acting on a personal belief that world conditions might improve if representatives of all nations fully understood the words being used in vital negotiations, I proposed a multilingual dictionary which would give exact definitions of key terms. The idea behind the dictionary was to clear up the problem of the AMBIGUITY that often developed in the course of negotiations between countries. Much to my surprise, however, a friend of mine who worked at the UN was very cool to the idea. "You have to understand," he explained, "that AMBIGUOUS words are extraordinarily important in negotiations. They are a face-saving device in sticky situations. You can always say, 'Oh, is <u>that</u> what you thought I meant,' and thereby avoid a lot of potentially embarrassing situations."

<u>Word Link:</u> VAGUE

<u>Memory Key:</u> The sentence I AM BIG, YOU US (AMBIGUOUS) is confusing and VAGUE. You don't know what it means.

ALLEGE ════════════════════════════════════
(auh LEDG)—to state something is true without proving it

In our country, a person is considered innocent until proven guilty, which helps to explain why we hear the word ALLEGE so often. ALLEGE is the word to use in situations in which there has been an accusation of wrongdoing but as yet no trial and no proof. A public official who is ALLEGED to have taken a bribe is someone who might be suspected of having been paid off, but this has not been proved as yet. There are other imaginative uses for the word. When an employer says that one of his employees is home with an ALLEGED illness, it's a safe bet the employer has his doubts about how sick the employee really is. And I once read a drama review in which the critic described the writer as an ALLEGED playwright. I don't think the writer was amused.

<u>Word Link:</u> SUSPECT

<u>Memory Key:</u> A murderer is SUSPECTED of pushing his victim off A LEDGE (ALLEGE).

PLAUSIBLE

(PLAW zuh b'l)—superficially believable; seeming to be true, convincing, or trustworthy

Somebody has just told you a remarkable story, insisting it's true. You have no proof that the story is indeed true, but you have no reason to doubt it either. In other words, the story is PLAUSIBLE —it could have occurred, it is superficially believable. The key to the word PLAUSIBLE isn't truth but the possibility of truth. A scientist who develops a PLAUSIBLE theory about the origin of the universe hasn't solved a mystery but has merely come up with an idea that sounds reasonable. Later perhaps new facts may call the theory into question.

Word Link: POSSIBLE

Memory Key: In order to make his high expense report more POSSIBLE, an executive submits his PLAZA BILL (PLAUSIBLE), his bill from the Hotel Plaza.

CODICIL

(COD i s'l)—a supplement, usually a later addition to a will modifying or revoking it

Let's say you want to make a change in your will. So rather than pay the expense of rewriting the entire legal document, you can add a CODICIL, a supplement, in which you state the modifications you want to make. There's a popular detective story in which expectations of the family members are high as they listen to a will until the lawyer comes to the CODICIL where the deceased revokes most of his bequests and leaves his money to someone outside the family. You can also use CODICIL to mean any kind of supplement or appendix to something that is written. In a way, it's similar to a postscript (P.S.) at the end of a letter. In a biography, the author added a CODICIL at the end of the book in which he gave some additional information which clarified a situation for the readers.

Word Link: ADDITION

Memory Key: To protect your house exterior, you might ADD a COAT OF SEAL (CODICIL).

Word Game

Fill in the blanks with the appropriate word from this section.

1. The nonguilty verdict indicated that the jury members found the defendant's story _____.

2. It is customary for the coroner to hold an _____ when someone dies under mysterious circumstances.

3. As soon as the district attorney accumulates enough evidence he intends to _____ the notorious mob leader.

4. The _____ statements of the witness seemed to confuse the jury.

5. The lawyer's contention was that there were circumstances that served to _____ the seriousness of his client's crime.

6. The judge was careful to _____ to the jury the precise procedure he wanted followed.

7. In the absence of his real father, the boy's uncle served as a _____ parent.

8. Falsifying the numbers on a cash register tape is an example of petty _____.

9. Without proof you can only _____ that a suspect has committed a crime.

10. The _____ to the will changed some minor bequests.

Answers: 1. plausible 2. inquest 3. indict 4. ambiguous 5. mitigate 6. stipulate 7. surrogate 8. larceny 9. allege 10. codicil

Word Game III

Match the word on the left with the proper definition on the right.

1. codicil	A. assert
2. mitigate	B. unclear
3. indict	C. charge
4. inquest	D. believable
5. larceny	E. hearing
6. allege	F. specify
7. stipulate	G. the crime of stealing
8. surrogate	H. make less severe
9. ambiguous	I. substitute
10. plausible	J. supplement

Answers: 1-J 2-H 3-C 4-E 5-G 6-A 7-F 8-I 9-B 10-D

Word Game ▯▯▯

Write the word link next to each word and see the image of the memory key in your mind.

1. plausible _____
2. allege _____
3. surrogate _____
4. inquest _____
5. ambiguous _____
6. mitigate _____
7. stipulate _____
8. indict _____
9. larceny _____
10. codicil _____

Answers: 1. possible 2. assert 3. substitute 4. death investigation 5. vague 6. lessen 7. specify 8. accuse 9. theft 10. supplement

Two Before Bedtime

Words like <u>myopia, placebo, prognosis,</u> and other terms in this section are second nature to anybody with any kind of medical background, but they are words with applications beyond medicine. When a politician, for instance, is accused of being <u>myopic,</u> a medical term for nearsightedness, it isn't the condition of his eyes that is being brought into question. It's his inability to see the long-range consequences of his actions. Nearly all the words in this section share with <u>myopia</u> a figurative distinction that has little to do with medicine.

prognosis
remission
traumatic
psychosomatic
chronic
congenital
hospice
incipient
myopia
placebo

PROGNOSIS

(prog NO sis)—forecast or prediction, especially of the probable course of an illness

Usually, but not always, we expect to hear a PROGNOSIS from a medical person. A surgeon operating on the knee of a football player will give sportswriters a PROGNOSIS as to the possible success of the operation: He may PROGNOSTICATE a speedy recovery or a lengthy convalescence. But you don't have to be a doctor to make a PROGNOSIS. Economists are forever offering PROGNOSES on how long inflation will be with us. And what is a weather forecaster but a person who gives us a daily PROGNO-SIS of the coming weather patterns?

Word Link: PREDICTION

Memory Key: A professional who is very good at making PREDIC-TIONS is a PRO who KNOWS how to SEE (PROGNOSIS).

REMISSION

(ri MISH un)—abatement, letup, cessation; pardon; cancellation of a debt

If, years ago, someone spoke to you about a REMISSION, chances are he was talking about pardon (a forgiveness), as in the religious phrase "remission of sins." Or it might have meant that, happily for you, your debts had been canceled.

Today, however, a REMISSION most often refers to a lessening or disappearance of the symptoms of a disease. But doctors are quick to point out that a REMISSION is not necessarily a cure. It could be simply a temporary condition. The word comes from the Latin remittere, "to send back." So, metaphorically, RE-MISSION means the illness has been sent back to where it came from.

Word Link: LETUP

Memory Key: A doctor named RAY is brought in on a case. RAY's MISSION (REMISSION): to bring about a LETUP in the patient's disease.

TRAUMATIC
(trow MAT ick)—relating to a wound or an emotional shock

"I had the most TRAUMATIC experience," my daughter was telling me not long ago. I braced for the worst but then was surprised, not to mention relieved, that what my daughter was describing as TRAUMATIC was merely a mildly embarrassing situation. This is a common enough practice: using TRAUMATIC as a synonym for "upsetting." But there's a big difference between a mildly embarrassing experience and a TRAUMATIC one. If you or I experience a genuine TRAUMA, the impact of it is going to be with us for quite a while. Generally, we use the adjective to describe a shock or injury that, with or without a physical effect, leaves a lasting mark on our minds.

Word Link: SHOCK

Memory Key: If a tic were capable of giving a SHOCK, it would be called a TRAUMA TIC (TRAUMATIC).

PSYCHOSOMATIC
(sigh ko so MAT ik)—pertaining to physical disorder caused by emotional stress

My father used to say that man was the only animal capable of talking his way into trouble. Now psychologists tell us that man is also capable of thinking himself into becoming sick. This brings up the word PSYCHOSOMATIC, used to describe any illness in which symptoms are produced, in part, by psychological or emotional factors. You should bear in mind that a PSYCHOSOMATIC illness is a real condition and not imagined. A stomach ulcer, for instance, may be caused by emotional stress but it shows up on an X ray and has to be treated like any physical illness. The word itself, as you may have already guessed, has a Greek origin, combining the Greek word for mind, psych, with the Greek word for body, soma.

Word Link: STRESS ILLNESS

Memory Key: A CYCLE in which you are SO MAD (PSYCHOSO-MATIC) so much of the time can cause STRESS ILLNESS.

CHRONIC ══════════════════════════════════════
(KRON ik)—continuous, constant, prolonged, recurring periodically.

Anytime you have a CHRONIC problem, whether it be with your back, your car, your television set, or a relative, you have a problem that you more or less have to live with, a problem that keeps recurring. This is not quite the same thing as having an acute problem, which describes a crisis that comes to a point quickly and intensely. Some CHRONIC problems, of course, are acute as well but not necessarily. CHRONIC bursitis is troublesome, but an acute bursitis attack is enough to send you to the doctor for a shot. The distinction is clear. Use CHRONIC when you want to suggest the idea of constant recurrence. Use acute when you want to convey the idea of urgency.

Word Link: CONSTANT

Memory Key: You had trouble sleeping last night because a CROW named NICK (CHRONIC) kept you up with his CONSTANT cawing.

CONGENITAL
(kon JEN uh t'l)—existing or dating from birth; innate, inborn, inbred

CONGENITAL is one of the more confusing words in English, the reason being that it has several conflicting meanings and is thus open to misinterpretation. Strictly speaking, CONGENITAL refers to the specific moment in which the embryo was conceived and the ensuing fetus growth period. It does not necessarily refer to heredity. A CONGENITAL deformity is a defect whose root cause can be linked to the period of gestation or the moment of birth but isn't necessarily related to the genetic mechanisms themselves.

That's one side of the confusion created by this word. The other side has to do with the common mistake of using this word interchangeably with words like habitual or ingrained. Some people will use the phrase CONGENITAL liar to describe a person who constantly (habitually) lies, but surely they're not saying that the person lies because of some event that occurred during pregnancy. I have an aunt who says she has a CONGENITAL dislike of cats. What she means is that she has an ingrained dislike of cats. The rule is simple: Use CONGENITAL only when you're referring to traits that can be traced back to the moment of birth or before.

Word Link: AT BIRTH

Memory Key: In talking about a young girl with a birth defect, you might ask the question: CAN JENNY TALK (CONGENITAL), or was she deaf and dumb AT BIRTH?

HOSPICE

(HOS pis)—shelter or lodging for travelers, the underprivileged, or sick, often maintained by a religious group

HOSPICE is a word seen more frequently today than in the past, mainly because there is something of a movement going on to form HOSPICES for people suffering from apparent terminal illnesses. Such HOSPICES combine the friendly and warm atmosphere of a home with the medical facilities of a small hospital.

Word Link: SHELTER

Memory Key: Eating a HOT SPICE (HOSPICE) sometimes makes your mouth feel as if it wants to run for SHELTER.

INCIPIENT

(in SIP ee ent)—beginning to be; about to appear

In contrast with the previous word congenital, there's no ambiguity with INCIPIENT's meaning. The connotation is specific. It refers to something that is just beginning, and you often hear it used medically. A child with a runny nose, for example, shows signs of an INCIPIENT cold. Outside medical circles it carries the same meaning. Violence in an Asian village could indicate an INCIPIENT (in the first stages) revolution. As a sailor I realize that when the wind backs from the southwest to the east, usually it's the sign of an INCIPIENT storm. I realize also I'd better head for the harbor since it also indicates an INCIPIENT seasickness for my wife.

Word Link: BEGINNING

Memory Key: The restaurant used to be so easy to get into in the BEGINNING that IN, ZIP WE WENT (INCIPIENT).

MYOPIA

(my OH pee a)—not able to see well in the distance; figuratively, not being able to see future possibilities

MYOPIA is one of a large family of words that has both a strict technical definition but can be used figuratively as well. If you have trouble seeing things at a distance, an ophthalmologist would describe you as being MYOPIC, that is, nearsighted, and would prescribe glasses. But if you were a politician and a columnist described you as MYOPIC, you'd probably take offense because what the columnist would be saying about you is that you lack the ability to see issues beyond their immediate significance. A person with a MYOPIC view of life, in other words, is someone who has trouble seeing beyond what is directly in front of him.

Word Link: SHORT SIGHT

Memory Key: In talking about a very tiny piano, you might say, "MY OWN PIANO (MYOPIA) is so SHORT I can't SEE it from a distance."

PLACEBO

(pluh SEE bow)—harmless pill

A good way to think of the word PLACEBO is as a bit of medical sleight of hand. Technically speaking, a PLACEBO is a pill made up of a harmless, unmedicated preparation. The person taking the pill, however, believes that he or she is actually taking medication. PLACEBOS are frequently used in experiments to test the effectiveness of a medication. One group of people will receive the substance being tested while another group is given the PLACEBO. I once participated in a test in which some of us were given large doses of vitamin C and others were given PLACEBOS. I don't know to this day which I had, but I felt better!

Word Link: PILL

Memory Key: Picture a violin bow on top of an aspirin bottle. What you have done is to PLACE the BOW (PLACEBO) on the PILL bottle.

Word Game

Write true or false next to the following statements:

1. A chronic condition is a condition that goes away for good once you treat it. ______
2. When a disease is in remission, the patient usually feels better. ______
3. A traumatic experience is easily forgotten. ______
4. Birth defects are an example of a congenital condition. ______
5. A person who can see clearly into the future could be called myopic. ______
6. Stress can produce psychosomatic illness. ______
7. Taking placebos can be dangerous to your health. ______
8. On the basis of an examination, a doctor can usually make an accurate prognosis. ______
9. At a hospice you're likely to find sick people. ______
10. A cold in its incipient stages has already run its course. ______

Answers: 1-F 2-T 3-F 4-T 5-F 6-T 7-F 8-T 9-T 10-F

Word Game ‖

Write the proper word next to its definition.

1. upsetting and emotionally shocking   _____

2. a forecast of things to come   _____

3. constant and prolonged   _____

4. innate, dating from birth   _____

5. nearsighted, unable to see well in the dis-
    tance   _____

6. a harmless pill   _____

7. just beginning to appear   _____

8. having both physical and psychological
    characteristics   _____

9. a retreat for sick people   _____

10. beginning to be or to appear   _____

Answers: 1. traumatic 2. prognosis 3. chronic 4. congenital
    5. myopic 6. placebo 7. incipient 8. psychosomatic 9. hospice
    10. incipient

Word Game ▯▯▯

Write the proper word next to its memory word link.

1. shock _____
2. prediction _____
3. constant _____
4. illness _____
5. birth _____
6. sight _____
7. pill _____
8. beginning _____
9. shelter _____
10. letup _____

Answers: 1. traumatic 2. prognosis 3. chronic 4. psychosomatic
     5. congenital 6. myopic 7. placebo 8. incipient 9. hospice
     10. remission

Review all memory keys before going on.

XI

Government Property

WEEK 2, DAY 4

You don't necessarily have to agree with everything our government does, but it's a good idea at least to understand what our politicians are saying. The ten words in this section are all words that you're likely to hear in a political speech or read about in a political article. Most of them, moreover, have applications outside the political arena as well.

surtax
bipartisan
amnesty
ideology
mandatory
moratorium
gerrymander
polity
conspiracy
demagogue

SURTAX

(SUR tax)—an extra or additional tax

Taxes are difficult enough to swallow, but a SURTAX adds insult to injury. It is a special tax above and beyond what you're already paying. Usually, SURTAX refers to a graduated income tax imposed on a company or individual whose income has passed a certain level. Much of the acrimony between large corporations and the government has to do with the government's desire to impose a SURTAX on excess company profits.

Word Link: ABOVE

Memory Key: Any tax ABOVE what a person normally pays in taxes is a SOUR TAX (SURTAX).

BIPARTISAN

(by PAR tuh zan)—representing or composed of two parties or groups

Take the word partisan, "supporter of a side," and prefix it with bi, meaning "two," and you end up with BIPARTISAN, a word suggesting support from two sides. When the President of the United States gets BIPARTISAN support on an issue, it means that he's getting the backing of both Democrats and Republicans. The word, of course, is useful only in nations in which there are two principal political factions.

Word Link: SUPPORT

Memory Key: You've brought two feuding factions together for a party and BY the PARTY'S END (BIPARTISAN) you hope to have the SUPPORT of both groups.

AMNESTY

(AM nes tee)—a general pardon by a government for past offenses

After the Vietnamese War, some congressmen argued that the government should grant AMNESTY to the young people who refused to serve after they were drafted. These congressmen, in other words, were asking the government to <u>forget</u> about what the young draft resisters had done. Or, to put it another way, they were asking the government to have an attack of <u>amnesia.</u>

AMNESTY and <u>amnesia</u>—the two words come from the same Greek root <u>amnasthai,</u> literally "not to remember." The first person in history to grant AMNESTY seems to have been a Greek general who said he would pardon his enemies and "not remember" their wrongs. Today, AMNESTY conveys the idea of a promise that an offense will be forgiven and officially forgotten. The word, however, is used mainly for groups of people and not for individuals.

<u>Word Link:</u> FORGET

<u>Memory Key:</u> Another way of saying you don't remember where you're living is "I FORGET where I AM NESTING (AMNESTY)."

IDEOLOGY

(i dee OL oh gee)—beliefs or ideas that form the basis of a political, economic, or social system

IDEOLOGY is a word that has taken a lot of twists and turns over the past 200 years. To early philosophers, the word was a good way to describe the science of ideas, in other words, philosophy. But Napoleon, in the eighteenth century, equated the word with dreamy, unrealistic theorizing. Napoleon wasn't using the word correctly, but he was, after all, an important figure so the meaning has stuck.

And where does this leave us today? Well, it's still proper to use the word when you're talking about a person's or a nation's belief system, as in the fact that IDEOLOGICAL differences separate the United States from the countries of Eastern Europe. But more and more the term has taken on a negative connotation. Columnist William Safire, for instance, has noted that in its current political use, IDEOLOGY is a "mental straitjacket for the philosophically narrow-minded."

Word Link: BELIEF

Memory Key: Something you might say to a pagan: "So you believe in an IDOL. OH, GEE (IDEOLOGY)!"

MANDATORY ═══════════════════════════════
(MAN da tor ee)—obligatory, compulsory; relating to an authoritative command, order, or injunction

Here's a word that doesn't fool around. It tells us that whatever action it describes is inescapably necessary and that no alternative can be considered for the moment. The meaning of MANDATORY overlaps with the meanings of the words compulsory and obligatory, but it's useful to keep in mind the differences. Compulsory suggests the idea that coercion and punishment will be used to enforce a rule. Obligatory implies that something is expected of us not so much by official command, but on the basis of conscience or a sense of moral obligation. MANDATORY seems to fall somewhere between these two synonyms. A good example of the entire sense of the word would be the idea of MANDATORY fuel rationing. It combines the official demand to cut back with a moral obligation to conserve energy.

A word closely related to MANDATORY is mandate, which suggests the authority inherited by a public official on the basis of a public vote on a specific issue. A politician who wins in a landslide is presumed to have a clear <u>mandate</u> to implement his programs.

<u>Word Link:</u> ORDER

<u>Memory Key:</u> The ORDER from the submarine captain was MAN THE TORpedoes (MANDATORY).

MORATORIUM
(mor uh TOR ee um)—legal authorization to delay payment or money due; waiting period

MORATORIUM is a useful word that works anytime you want to suggest a temporary delay of some specified activity. In politics the word is often used to suggest a truce, as in a MORATORIUM on criticism of foreign policy. In a section of my town, the planning board imposed a MORATORIUM on building new homes until a better sewage system could be devised. And if you should ever find yourself in a severe financial bind, a good strategy is to see if you can get your creditors to give you a MORATORIUM on payments until you get back on your feet again.

<u>Word Link:</u> DELAY

<u>Memory Key:</u> The speechmaker was ordered not to DELAY singing anyMORE of his ORATORY HYMNS (MORATORIUM).

GERRYMANDER
(JER ee mander)—to alter a voting district unfairly

What a curious word! Coined around 1812 and used today strictly as a political term, GERRYMANDER owes its place in our language to a man named Elbridge Gerry who was the governor of Massachusetts in 1812. It seems that while Gerry was in office, the Massachusetts legislature, in an effort to gain better control of elections, rearranged the shape of Essex County. When they were finished the new district resembled a salamander. A clever newspaper editor at the time combined Gerry's name with salamander to create a term that describes the reshaping of political districts for political advantage.

Word Link: RESHAPE

Memory Key: To fit a doorway at home, you might want to RESHAPE a GERMAN DOOR (GERRYMANDER).

POLITY ══════════════════════════════════════
(POL uh tee)—a system or form of government

POLITY is a straightforward word and is the form or type of government of a nation, state, church, or any kind of institution. The POLITY of the United States, for example, is a representative democracy. The sovereignty resides ultimately in us the people, who elect others to represent us. The POLITY of Saudi Arabia is a kingdom.

In the test phrase "They made a POLITY," 66 percent of college seniors incorrectly believed the word meant "pact," according to Johnson O'Connor. He went on to say that a POLITY may be the result of a pact or agreement, but it is the structure of government. POLITY also differs from policy, for policy refers to the management of a government, while POLITY is confined to its makeup.

Word Link: GOVERNMENT

Memory Key: Our cat changed the GOVERNMENT on our farm and had the parrot POLLY IN for TEA (POLITY) to talk over its structure.

CONSPIRACY

(kun SPIR uh see)—a criminal or treasonable plan; collusion; plot

CONSPIRACY is used broadly to cover a variety of circumstances. Basically it denotes a secret agreement between people to commit an unlawful act. But don't confuse CONSPIRACY with the act itself. From time to time, for instance, you might read that the government has indicted a group of business firms manufacturing a similar product in a CONSPIRACY to control prices. CONSPIRACY here refers to the secret agreement to control the price, collusion. Several people in an organization might CONSPIRE to make sure their candidate wins the nomination. And a CONSPIRACY against the government is linked with treasonable acts such as overthrowing the present regime. A notable CONSPIRACY trial took place in the United States (1806) when Aaron Burr, a famous soldier, patriot, and politician, was tried for treason against the government.

Word Link: PLOT

Memory Key: CAN SPIRO SEE (CONSPIRACY) the PLOT against him?

DEMAGOGUE

(DEM uh gog)—political agitator; one who plays on emotions and prejudices to gain power

Time was when DEMAGOGUE meant a leader of the people, one who championed popular causes. This was a direct translation from the Greek. Today, however, we use DEMAGOGUE to describe an unprincipled leader who tries to capitalize on social discontent, appealing to the worst side of people, inflaming their emotions. Then again, one man's DEMAGOGUE is another man's patriot! Prior to the American Revolution, the British branded Tom

Paine, the American writer and patriot, as a DEMAGOGUE. True, Paine's powerful words helped to spark the revolution, but he had no desire for personal power.

Some people use DEMAGOGUE interchangeably with <u>dictator</u>. You shouldn't. A DEMAGOGUE may want to become a <u>dictator</u> and a <u>dictator</u> at times may act like a DEMAGOGUE, but the words are not synonymous.

<u>Word Link:</u> AGITATOR

<u>Memory Key:</u> The leader's AGITATING antics before the large crowd left THEM AGOG (DEMAGOGUE).

Word Game 🄸

Match the definition on the left with the proper word on the right.

1. alter unfairly	A. ideology
2. make obligatory	B. gerrymander
3. basis of political system	C. moratorium
4. general pardon	D. mandatory
5. added tax	E. bipartisan
6. two-party support	F. amnesty
7. legal delay	G. surtax
8. conspiracy	H. polity
9. political state	I. demagogue
10. political agitator	J. collusion

Answers: 1-B 2-D 3-A 4-F 5-G 6-E 7-C 8-J 9-H 10-I

Word Game II

Fill in the blank with the appropriate word from this section:

1. As the result of his meeting, the president was able to attract _____ support from Congress.

2. The two leaders split on the basis of differences in _____ _____.

3. After his election, the premier declared _____ for all political prisoners.

4. One of the ways a government can raise additional revenue is to impose a _____.

5. The legislature was criticized for its attempt to _____ ____ certain election districts.

6. The negotiators declared a _____ on information to the press.

7. There was nothing _____ about the President's suggestion.

8. The FBI discovered the _____ just in time.

9. The _____ whipped up the crowd to a frenzy.

10. Unfortunately, the situation was in the hands of a military _____.

Answers: 1. bipartisan 2. ideology 3. amnesty 4. surtax 5. gerry-mander 6. moratorium 7. mandatory 8. conspiracy 9. dema-gogue 10. polity

Word Game ⅢⅠ

Write the proper word next to its word link and visualize the memory key.

1. belief _____
2. forget _____
3. reshape _____
4. delay _____
5. double support _____
6. above _____
7. order _____
8. government _____
9. plot _____
10. agitator _____

Answers: 1. ideology 2. amnesty 3. gerrymander 4. moratorium
5. bipartisan 6. surtax 7. mandatory 8. polity 9. conspiracy
10. demagogue

XII
People's Choice

WEEK 2, DAY 5

Our legislation has contributed more than its share of memorable people and momentous events to American history, and so it's no surprise that politics has been the source of some of the more colorful and interesting words in our language. In this section we'll look at ten words that relate in one way or another to our political process. One of them, scapegoat, has its origins in biblical times, while another, telegenic, is such a new word that most dictionaries don't list it. All the words, I'm happy to say, are fair game for anybody, regardless of party affiliation.

telegenic
constituent
incumbent
consensus
populist
scapegoat
hustings
caucus
filibuster
plebeian

TELEGENIC
(tel uh JEN ic)—attractive on television

There's an expression in the entertainment industry that certain actors who look well on film are "eaten up by the camera." It's another way of saying the camera likes what it sees. These people project, they come across. Nearly all the top stars of television today have an unmistakable TELEGENIC quality. Politicians know that TELEGENIC appeal is vital to their campaigns and do whatever they can to please the camera and, consequently, the audience. The word is so new to our language you won't find it in most dictionaries. It comes from Greek tele, "far off," and genic, "producing, born."

Word Link: TELEVISION APPEAL

Memory Key: It's important for an anchorman to APPEAL to the InTELLIGENT (TELEGENIC) on TELEVISION.

CONSTITUENT
(con STITCH ew ent)—voter represented by an elected official

The first recorded use of the word CONSTITUENT as a term referring to voters came in the late 1760s in England, and, in many ways, the word symbolizes the tradition of representative government that our country inherited from England. A CONSTITUENT is a citizen who elected somebody else to represent him or her in government. As an adjective, the word suggests the right we all have as voters to be part of a CONSTITUENT group or a CONSTITUENT assembly with powers to produce political change.

Word Link: VOTE

Memory Key: The CONSTITUTION (CONSTITUENT) guarantees our right to VOTE.

INCUMBENT

(in KUM bent)—currently in office

INCUMBENT is one of those English words that gives foreigners learning English fits because of the number of ways it can be used. As a noun, the word refers to a politician who is holding office at the time of an election campaign. The INCUMBENT (the one in office) usually has a major elective advantage over his competitors. When you use the word as an adjective, it changes its meaning altogether and conveys the idea of a moral obligation or duty, as in the sentence, "It is INCUMBENT upon all of us to obey the government's fuel conservation program."

Word Link: OFFICEHOLDER and OBLIGATION

Memory Key: An OFFICEHOLDER IN A CONVENT (INCUMBENT) has an OBLIGATION to live a pure life.

CONSENSUS

(kon SEN sus)—general agreement, majority opinion, common consent

It's one thing to win the unanimous support of a group on a particular issue, and something else again to win only CONSENSUS support. When a group comes to a CONSENSUS about a plan, it means that most, but not all, of the people in the group agree. CONSENSUS is an important word in U.S. political affairs since politicians tend to act in accordance with the CONSENSUS feeling of their constituents. Not everyone, however, is convinced that CONSENSUS is the best way to conduct public affairs. There is a feeling that a dangerous CONSENSUS mentality of the public has been molded by the manipulations of mass communications.

Word Link: AGREE

Memory Key: Someone who has given their CONSENT to US (CONSENSUS) has AGREED to a desire of ours.

POPULIST

(POP you list)—a rural progressive desiring greater government participation

The word POPULIST first appeared in everyday conversation in the 1890s with the founding of the POPULIST party, a political group that championed the rights of workers in general and farmers in particular. The party was instrumental in the election of a number of congressmen, governors, and minor government officials in the mid-1890s, but almost disappeared from American life by the turn of the century. The term, however, lives on. When used with a small p, the term POPULIST is used to describe candidates and positions that favor the so-called little man and demand a more direct role of the federal government in everyday affairs.

Word Link: LITTLE MAN

Memory Key: If he's short, the POP YOU LIST (POPULIST) as your favorite parent is a LITTLE MAN.

SCAPEGOAT

(SCAPE goat)—whipping boy; someone who bears the blame for another

SCAPEGOAT is one word whose origin should make an indelible imprint on your mind. According to the Bible, on the Hebrew Day of Atonement, Aaron symbolically laid the sins of the people on the head of a goat and sent the goat into the wilderness. At the same time, a second goat was sacrificed to the Lord. In translating this section of the Bible into English, Tindale, in 1530, wrote the following: "And Aaron cast lottes over the two gootes; one lotte for the Lorde, and another for a scape-goat." Hence, the term SCAPEGOAT, someone who is blamed or punished for the wrong-doings of somebody else.

Word Link: BLAME

Memory Key: A goat has disappeared and you want to know who is to BLAME for the ESCAPE of the GOAT (SCAPEGOAT).

HUSTINGS
(HUS tings)—political campaigning

HUSTINGS, a word you can use synonymously with campaign trails, has had a curious etymological history. Originally, in Scandinavia and England, the word described a council or assembly brought together to deliberate serious matters. In England, it became the term used to describe a platform in a meeting hall on which the mayor and alderman took their seats, later becoming the temporary platform on which candidates for Parliament would stand and address the electorate. It's from this last usage that we derive the word's current meaning, since to be on the HUSTINGS (i.e., on a platform addressing the electorate) means being on the campaign trail.

Word Link: POLITICAL CAMPAIGN

Memory Key: HOUSE STING (HUSTINGS) is something a CAMPAIGNING POLITICIAN might receive if he knocked on the door of a beehive.

CAUCUS

(KAW kus)—a meeting of members of a political party to choose candidates or determine policy

A CAUCUS is a political meeting and an important ingredient in the American political scene. From local or regional CAUCUSES of party members, candidates for a political office are nominated and delegates chosen for nominating conventions. During presidential election years, CAUCUSES become news items inasmuch as a candidate's current popularity is reflected in the votes of the various state CAUCUSES.

Legislators may also call a CAUCUS to make party plans and decide on policy as well as possible candidates and appointees.

CAUCUS comes from caucauascu, an American Indian word in the Algonquian language meaning "elder" or "counselor." Out of our vocabulary of a million words or so, it is one of the few that comes from our Native Americans.

Word Link: MEETING

Memory Key: A loud MEETING might be called a RAUCOUS (CAUCUS).

FILIBUSTER

(FIL uh bus ter)—delaying tactics, such as long, irrelevant speeches to obstruct legislation

The FILIBUSTER is an American political invention, and a political phenomenon exclusive to the U.S. Senate. Because Rule 22 of the Senate permits unlimited debate on any measure before it can be brought to a vote, a minority of senators can prevent passage of or alter a bill through prolonged speeches. When the senators run out of information about the subject they're debating, they can turn to a telephone book and simply read out the names—anything to wear down the opposition. Until 1957, southern senators were able to defeat proposed civil rights legislation by just such FILIBUSTERING tactics. One method to end a FILIBUSTER is by cloture (KLOchur), in which debate is stopped by a two-thirds vote.

Word Link: LONG SPEECH

Memory Key: You can fall asleep during the LONG SPEECHES that sometimes FILL A BUS TOUR (FILIBUSTER).

PLEBEIAN ═══════════════════════════════════
(pli BEE an)—vulgar, common, uncultured

PLEBEIAN is an insulting word. By calling someone PLEBEIAN you're saying he's without any sense of style or taste, whether it's in clothes, reading material, art, home decoration, or the like. But all of us, I suppose, have PLEBEIAN tendencies in one way or another. A friend of mine favors a particular brand of ketchup. Whenever he goes to a restaurant, expensive or otherwise, he always insists on this ketchup, putting it on everything he eats— fish, potatoes, vegetables. Once when I was with him I heard an outraged French maitre d' mumble under his breath, "Such PLEBEIAN American taste!" The meaning of PLEBEIAN is directly related to its Latin origin, plebeius, "of the people," and especially referred to the riffraff of Roman society. It seems they weren't expected to have the same tastes as those who ruled.

Word Link: VULGAR (uncultured)

Memory Key: The critic dismissed the PLAY as BEING (PLEBEIAN) VULGAR.

Word Game [

Match the words in the left-hand column with the synonyms in the right-hand column.

1. hustings	A. attractive on television
2. scapegoat	B. majority opinion
3. incumbent	C. whipping boy
4. telegenic	D. currently holding office
5. consensus	E. campaign trail
6. populist	F. represented voter
7. constituent	G. of the common people
8. plebeian	H. delaying tactics
9. caucus	I. meeting of political party
10. filibuster	J. vulgar

Answers: 1-E 2-C 3-D 4-A 5-B 6-G 7-F 8-J 9-I 10-H

Word Game ⫿

Write true or false after the following statements:

1. If you had <u>consensus</u> support within a group, you would have trouble getting people to back you. _____

2. <u>Telegenic</u> political candidates have a certain advantage over their nontelegenic opponents. _____

3. In 1972, Richard Nixon was the <u>incumbent</u> presidential candidate. _____

4. A candidate with <u>populist</u> appeal generally has the support of only the very rich. _____

5. Nearly all Americans can call themselves <u>constituents.</u> _____

6. <u>Scapegoats</u> are always the guilty party. _____

7. Nearly all politicians find themselves on the <u>hustings</u> at one time or another. _____

8. An aristocrat comes from a <u>plebeian</u> family. _____

9. The <u>filibuster</u> effectively prevented the measure from being adopted. _____

10. A <u>caucus</u> has nothing to do with the appointing of delegates. _____

Answers: 1-F 2-T 3-T 4-F 5-T 6-F 7-T 8-F 9-T 10-F

Word Game ▯▯▯

Write the correct word next to its word link and get an image of the memory key at the same time.

1. meeting _____

2. interminable speech _____

3. television _____

4. agreement _____

5. common man _____

6. blame _____

7. campaign _____

8. voter _____

9. office _____

10. vulgar _____

Answers: 1. caucus 2. filibuster 3. telegenic 4. consensus 5. populist 6. scapegoat 7. hustings 8. constituent 9. incumbent 10. plebeian

TEST II

You are now halfway through the book. In this test you will be able to measure the increase of your word memory power more accurately. Select the definition you believe is the correct answer. Write it down; then go to the end of the test to check your results.

1. populist A. political straddler B. rural progressive C. birth control advocate
2. incipient A. beginning B. unnoticed C. exhausted
3. placebo A. familiar location B. harmless pill C. peace offering
4. mandatory A. despotic B. optional C. obligatory
5. ambiguous A. not clear B. long-winded C. able to use with equal ease
6. chronic A. widespread B. cranky C. continuous
7. quixotic A. eccentric B. foolishly romantic C. illusive
8. carte blanche A. unrestricted authority B. eloquence C. strictness
9. graffiti A. heavy-handed vulgarity B. dishonesty C. wall scribblings
10. indict A. accuse B. disapprove C. rebuke
11. plausible A. evasive B. practicable C. possibly true

12. allege A. assert without proof B. offer a suggestion C. promise solemnly
13. prognosis A. preference B. identification of a disease C. forecast
14. remission A. neglect B. abatement C. refusal to listen
15. amnesty A. international agreement B. diplomatic immunity C. pardon
16. surtax A. penalty B. partial payment C. extra tax
17. incumbent A. negotiator B. officeholder C. oppressor
18. scapegoat A. whipping boy B. dishonest person C. lost animal
19. myopia A. farsighted B. fussy C. nearsighted
20. bipartisan A. narrow-minded B. separated into parts C. representing two parties
21. telegenic A. attractive on television B. scientifically inclined C. sense of the future
22. hospice A. gift B. fiesta C. shelter
23. moratorium A. security for a debt B. delay C. funeral home
24. stipulate A. specify B. undertake C. suggest
25. mitigate A. to prolong B. persuade C. moderate
26. psychosomatic involving A. extrasensory perception B. body language C. body and mind
27. larceny A. deception B. hedging C. theft
28. cachet A. hiding place B. basket C. prestige
29. kowtow A. fawn B. smile C. give a karate chop
30. modus operandi A. hi-fi unit B. large computer C. procedure
31. inquest A. deposition B. arrest C. investigation
32. congenital A. dating from birth B. extremely friendly C. original or primitive
33. surrogate A. authenticated B. protected C. substitute
34. status quo A. character B. flat statement C. existing condition
35. constituent related to: A. strength B. voting C. agreement
36. hustings A. flashy activity B. political campaigning C. elaborate procedures
37. sine qua non A. something indispensable B. high achievement C. whatever is absent

38. traumatic A. paralysis B. blockage C. shock
39. ideology A. beliefs B. creativeness C. image worship
40. gerrymander A. be fickle B. invalidate C. alter unfairly
41. incommunicado A. closemouthed B. in solitary confinement C. disguised
42. consensus A. presentation of main points B. recommendation C. general agreement
43. conspiracy A. propaganda B. plot C. slander
44. filibuster A. delaying tactics B. one who trains young horses C. unfair tactics
45. polity A. courtesy B. political state C. court of justice
46. contretemps A. excitement B. mistake C. dishonesty
47. codicil A. tabulation B. summary C. supplement
48. demagogue A. one advocating violence B. dictator C. political agitator
49. plebeian A. narrow-minded B. argumentative C. vulgar
50. caucus A. political meeting B. poll C. mock trial

Answers: 1-B 2-A 3-B 4-C 5-A 6-C 7-B 8-A 9-C 10-A 11-C 12-A 13-C 14-B 15-C 16-C 17-B 18-A 19-C 20-C 21-A 22-C 23-B 24-A 25-C 26-C 27-C 28-C 29-A 30-C 31-C 32-A 33-C 34-C 35-B 36-B 37-A 38-C 39-A 40-C 41-B 42-C 43-B 44-A 45-B 46-B 47-C 48-C 49-C 50-A

These fifty words are vital ones for you to know. They are not always easy, even with the memory links. If you find you have a score of 30 or less correct, spend a few days reviewing the words you missed and you will put them close to your active memory center.

XIII

Meaty Modifiers

WEEK 3, DAY 1

Given a choice, would you rather get advice that was <u>pithy</u> or <u>cryptic?</u> And how would you feel if you were a writer whose stories were described by a critic as being <u>mundane?</u> Each of these three words, as well as all the words in this section, are adjectives, that is, modifiers. But they are adjectives that pack a good deal of power. They do more than simply modify: They tell a story.

pithy
tenuous
cryptic
internecine
cogent
graphic
mundane
inexorable
obtuse
pejorative

PITHY ————————————————————
(PITH ee)—succinct, concise; having substance and point; terse
and full of significance

A child was standing in the monkey house of a zoo and asked a
man nearby why there were so many different types of monkeys.
The child didn't know when he asked the question that the man
was a zoologist. After a half hour of detailed explanation the child
said, "Thank you, but that's more than I wanted to know about
monkeys!" Had he known better, he could have made a point of
asking for a PITHY explanation.

    PITHY means, literally, "full of <u>pith</u>," the essential tissue at the
center of a plant's stem or the vital marrow in a bone. This is why
a PITHY reply or a PITHY argument is one that is packed with
meaning and substance, with no wasted words—and no unnecessary monkey business.

<u>Word Link:</u> CONCISE

<u>Memory Key:</u> If you put a dictionary inside a hat worn by jungle
explorers, you'd have a PITH (PITHY) helmet filled with CONCISE
and concentrated meanings.

TENUOUS ————————————————————
(TEN you us)—slender, thin, unsubstantial

TENUOUS is one of those words whose everyday usage has
become less and less precise in recent years. Today the word is
used most frequently to imply instability or weakness, as in a
TENUOUS truce in a part of the world where truces do not last for
very long. Strictly speaking, however, the primary meaning of the
word is slender in the sense of lines, wires, or cords. Weakness
is not necessarily implied. Thus you can describe as TENUOUS
the wires holding heavy mobile sculptures in museums and not

worry that the sculptures are going to fall on your head. And don't try to convince a wasp or a fly that the TENUOUS filaments of a spider's web are not very strong.

A versatile word, TENUOUS can be applied accurately in such varied situations as film criticism, dismissing a film because its plot is too TENUOUS (vague, hazy, etc.), or to a lawyer's arsenal when he pleads EXTENUATING (thinning out) circumstances to make a bad action seem less severe.

Word Link: THIN

Memory Key: If you had ten female sheep who hadn't eaten in a week, you'd have TEN EWES (TENUOUS) who were very THIN.

CRYPTIC
(KRIP tik)—having a hidden meaning; puzzling, mysterious

Originally, a CRYPT meant a hidden cave or a burial place, and although it refers specifically to an underground room beneath the main floor of a church, the "hidden" aspect of the meaning remains when we use the word as an adjective. A CRYPTIC message, in short, is one in which the real meaning of what is said is hidden and you have to "read between the lines" to decipher the intended meaning.

Word Link: HIDDEN

Memory Key: Someone has hidden a wind-up alarm clock inside a crib. You can hear the ticking but you can't see the clock, so the HIDDEN clock makes it seem as if the CRIB is TICKing (CRYPTIC).

INTERNECINE

(in tur NEE seen)—deadly; mutually destructive; relating to feuds and squabbles within a group

INTERNECINE at one time was a word confined to the description of bloody civil wars or those violent frontier feuds in which members of one family would try to kill members of another family. Today, though, the word can be applied to just about any type of internal power struggle or feud, whether there is violence or not. An INTERNECINE struggle for power and influence often takes place in government, institutions, and business.

Word Link: FAMILY FEUD

Memory Key: When birds get into a FAMILY FEUD, the result is an INNER NESt SCENE (INTERNECINE) of squabbling.

COGENT

(KO jent)—compelling; forcible; urgent

COGENT is a tough, powerful 45-caliber word—so much so that mathematicians might think of the word as a number raised to the nth degree, that is, the utmost degree. If you can present COGENT reasons for taking a particular action, few people are going to argue with you. How could they in the face of reasons so validly convincing and persuasive? Remember the Three Mile Island nuclear disaster? Aren't we given COGENT reasons for reexamining the potential dangers of nuclear power plants?

Word Link: CONVINCE

Memory Link: Think of the old Telly Savalas character, Kojak, a New York police lieutenant. When Kojak had a point to make, he usually did it in a CONVINCING, COGENT way, a KOJAK (COGENT) cop.

GRAPHIC
(GRAPH ik)—vivid, striking; described with pictorial effect

GRAPHIC comes to us from the Greek word grapho, "to write or draw," a word that has spawned a host of familiar words, such as telegraph, "writing over a long distance," or photograph, which means literally "a 'light' drawing." The word comes in handy when we want to describe an event with an added measure of clarity or brilliance. James Herriot's books are an amusing, charming, and highly GRAPHIC description of a veterinarian's life in rural England. Why is it so GRAPHIC? Because you can actually see in your mind the countryside and the characters. The book stimulates your mind's eye in a way that not even television can surpass.

Word Link: SEE

Memory Key: Picture a typical graph. Think to yourself, The GRAPH I SEE. And what is GRAPHIC but the word GRAPH with the letters I and C.

MUNDANE
(mun DANE)—ordinary, worldly

MUNDANE is a word with a negative connotation it does not deserve. Most of us are more MUNDANE than we realize and we have nothing to be ashamed of. The word is a neutral one and merely refers to the ordinary rounds of everyday activities—struggling out of bed in the morning, eating, making a living, shopping, laundry, all the commonplace, practical, and sometimes humdrum aspects of life. Since a MUNDANE activity is apt to be transitory, it tends to contrast our daily life with whatever seems eternal or more spiritual, romantic, idealistic. Consequently, it has acquired a negative sense as something unworthy or inferior and some people use it as a verbal weapon to belittle or disdain, as "You're only interested in MUNDANE things." If the accuser means materialism and power, the word is used incorrectly.

Word Link: DAY-TO-DAY

Memory Key: MONday, to most of us, means back to the DAY-TO-DAY grind. Oh, those MUNDANE MONDAYS.

INEXORABLE
(in EK so ru b'l)—unyielding; relentless

INEXORABLE is one of the strongest words you'll ever come upon, so handle it with care. Just take a look at how many strong synonyms for the word are listed in Roget's Thesaurus: immovable, relentless, obdurate, inflexible, determined, irresistible, adamant, resolute, intractable, stubborn, steadfast, staunch, firm, uncooperative. None of these words really gives a precise meaning to INEXORABLE, but collectively they give us a keen sense of the brute force of the word.

I use INEXORABLE only when I want to convey the notion of "iron-willed" finality, as: With an INEXORABLE determination the explorer brought his expedition through a situation everyone believed was hopeless. Of course, you don't have to confine the word to people. Consider what is happening to the shoreline on many of our beaches, how it is giving way to the INEXORABLE inroads of the ocean.

Word Link: UNRELENTING

Memory Key: Imagine how horrible it would be to live with a pain so unrelenting it never went away. What is horrible about UNRELENTING pain is that it's INEXORABLE (in-EX-HORRIBLE).

OBTUSE

(ob TUSE)—dull; not sensitive or observant; slow-witted

It's always entertaining for me to trace the history of words that begin their career as practical descriptions of a concrete object or situation, and then generations later end up figuratively portraying a human quality. Take OBTUSE, which comes from the Latin obtundere and means "to beat on" or "to make dull as the edge of an ax or knife." If you've mowed lawns you know that at the end of a season of cutting grass and inadvertently striking stones, etc., the blade of your lawn mower becomes dull. Figuratively, that's the way it is with OBTUSE people. Their minds have a dull edge and have difficulty "cutting" through to anything that takes a reasonable amount of thought or sensitivity. They don't have the emotional and intellectual capacity to respond, which makes them seem slow or stupid. Most of us have had the frustrating experience of trying to explain something to an OBTUSE person. On the other hand, perhaps part of the problem may be in our presentation!

Because of the sound of the word, people tend to confuse OBTUSE with abstruse, which means profound or so difficult it is hard to understand.

Word Link: DULL

Memory Key: Another way of describing a boring poker hand is a DULL pair OF TWO's (OBTUSE).

PEJORATIVE

(pe JOR uh tiv)—to have a worsening effect; disparaging; derogatory

Many people know of the word PEJORATIVE, but are not sure how to use it. So they don't. The closest synonyms are depreciative, "something written or spoken that tends to lower the value or status of a thing," disparaging, which means "to belittle or to speak of as having small value or importance," and derogatory. When former President Carter held a press conference to talk about his new secretary of state, he noted that Edmund Muskie would be more creative and a stronger presence than his predecessor, which should evoke a positive response from foreign heads of state. This was a PEJORATIVE statement because it lowered the status of the former secretary, Cyrus Vance.

There is another sense in which you can use PEJORATIVE. As you know, some words shift in meaning over a period of time. Those that once were of a complimentary nature but now have acquired a derogatory implication have taken on what is called a PEJORATIVE meaning. For example, the modern meaning of egregious as something outstandingly bad (as in an egregious mistake) is a PEJORATIVE change from the original meaning of "distinguished" or "excellent."

Word Link: BELITTLE

Memory Key: Picture a PITCHER OF TEA (PEJORATIVE) shrinking to BE LITTLE (BELITTLE).

Word Game

Write the proper word next to its definition.

1. compelling and forceful   _____

2. unyielding and relentless   _____

3. thin and unsubstantial   _____

4. succinct and full of meaning   _____

5. vivid and striking   _____

6. puzzling, mysterious   _____

7. everyday and earthbound   _____

8. mutually destructive   _____

9. making worse   _____

10. dull   _____

Answers: 1. cogent 2. inexorable 3. tenuous 4. pithy 5. graphic
    6. cryptic 7. mundane 8. internecine 9. pejorative 10. obtuse

Word Game ⏸

Write true or false next to the following statements:

1. A <u>pithy</u> statement is usually wordy and pointless.   _____

2. Political parties are sometimes struck by <u>internecine</u> feuds.   _____

3. A parachute jump would be considered a <u>mundane</u> activity.   _____

4. A person with an <u>inexorable</u> opinion on a subject is easily swayed.   _____

5. A good debater knows how to make <u>cogent</u> arguments.   _____

6. A <u>cryptic</u> message is likely to confuse you.   _____

7. <u>Graphic</u> statements usually leave a great deal to the imagination.   _____

8. <u>Tenuous</u> materials are characterized by strength and substance.   _____

9. A sarcastic remark often has a <u>pejorative</u> effect in a disagreement.   _____

10. An <u>obtuse</u> student has difficulty with his courses.   _____

Answers: 1-F 2-T 3-F 4-F 5-T 6-T 7-F 8-F 9-T 10-T

Word Game □□□

Match the word in the left-hand column with its memory word link in the right-hand column.

1. graphic	A. concise
2. pithy	B. convince
3. inexorable	C. see
4. internecine	D. thin
5. cogent	E. family feud
6. mundane	F. hidden
7. tenuous	G. unrelenting
8. cryptic	H. day-to-day
9. pejorative	I. dull
10. obtuse	J. belittle

Answers: 1-C 2-A 3-G 4-E 5-B 6-H 7-D 8-F 9-J 10-I

MEMORY KEY REVIEW

Go back to the first list. Take each word individually and make sure you have a sharp picture in your mind of each memory key. (Note: Repeat this procedure at the end of each daily section.)

XIV

Mistaken Identity

WEEK 3, DAY 2

A comedian named Norm Crosby makes a career out of deliberately butchering the language, but he misuses words so smoothly he almost makes you believe he's in command of a rich and esoteric vocabulary. Each of the words listed above receives more than its share of misuse, too, but not deliberately. Because each has a near twin, the words above are often used interchangeably with their similar-looking and similar-sounding mate. Let's look at each set and see if, once and for all, we can clear up the distinctions.

presentiment
presentment

credible
creditable

appraise
apprise

affect
effect

presumptive
presumptuous

PRESENTIMENT

(pri ZEN tuh ment)—premonition, foreboding

PRESENTMENT

(pre ZENT ment)—presentation, the act of presenting a formal statement of a legal matter in a court

Here are two words differentiated by only the one letter i. Yet their meanings are worlds apart. In using them, be careful!

If you've ever had, without any apparent reason, a vague apprehension that something was about to go wrong, that is, a gut feeling, an instinctive or superstitious awareness, you've had a PRESENTIMENT. The basic idea behind the word is to see or feel something ahead of time.

What about PRESENTMENT? Well, chances are unless you're a lawyer or have otherwise spent much time in a courtroom, you're not familiar with the word. What it refers to, simply, is the act of presenting or laying before the court or person in authority a formal statement of some matter to be dealt with legally.

PRESENTIMENT

Word Link: TROUBLE AHEAD

Memory Key: PRESENT TORMENT (PRESENTIMENT) usually means TROUBLE AHEAD.

PRESENTMENT

Word Link: COURT

Memory Link: A gift shown in evidence to a COURT could be called a PRESENT MEANT (PRESENTMENT) to prove a person guilty.

CREDIBLE

(KRED uh b'l)—believable, plausible, trustworthy

CREDITABLE

(KRED it tuh b'l)—deserving credit or esteem, praiseworthy

These two words have the same Latin parent, which possibly explains why they are so frequently—and mistakenly—used interchangeably. The essence of CREDIBLE is believability. The man who promised to fix your roof didn't show up on the designated day, but the explanation he gave was CREDIBLE enough so that you're willing to believe his promise that he'll show up tomorrow. In other words, you believe him.

There's an element of belief in CREDITABLE as well, but an explanation can be CREDIBLE, that is, believeable, without being CREDITABLE, which means worthy of credit or esteem. When a contestant ran the Boston Marathon in 2 hours, 12 minutes, and 11 seconds, a newscaster called the feat a CREDITABLE performance, and if you know anything about distance, you know that the newscaster's description of Roger's feat was CREDIBLE.

CREDIBLE

Word Link: BELIEVE

Memory Key: If Congress were to CREATE a BILL (CREDIBLE) that put severe penalties on lying, we could then better BELIEVE our legislators.

CREDITABLE

Word Link: WORTHY

<u>Memory Key:</u> To a banker, a person who is CREDIT ABLE (CRED-ITABLE) is WORTHY of lending money to.

APPRAISE
(uh PRAZ)—to estimate, evaluate, determine the worth or merit of

APPRISE
(uh PRIZ)—to inform, give notice to, tell

If you frequently confuse these two words, you've got company. In fact, I was once the guest of a radio interviewer who berated me incorrectly because she was convinced I'd been careless in giving two different definitions to the same word in a book I'd written.

APPRAISE is often used interchangeably with <u>estimate,</u> but it has a wider application. An <u>estimate</u> can be either a casual <u>or</u> a professional evaluation, but when you get something AP-PRAISED, you're seeking an accurate, expert judgment. AP-PRAISE, in other words, is a stronger, more precise word than <u>estimate.</u>

APPRISE is a word I mention, not to encourage its usage, but rather to limit the situations in which you use it. The word is most frequently used in legal situations, in which a suspect is AP-PRISED, that is, notified, of his or her rights. The word is used most often in courts, so stick with simple words like <u>notify, inform,</u> or <u>advise.</u> Whatever you do, don't ask anybody to APPRISE the value of a gold necklace. He may turn around and APPRAISE you, for you would have made a mistake.

APPRAISE

<u>Word Link:</u> VALUE

Memory Key: One way to receive a good deal OF PRAISE (AP-PRAISE) is to do something that has VALUE to society.

APPRISE

Word Link: INFORM

Memory Key: You find out you've won A PRIZE (APPRISE). Now you want to be INFORMED about the nature of the prize.

AFFECT ————————————————————————
(uh FEKT)—to influence; produce a noticeable reaction, response, or change

EFFECT ————————————————————————
(i FEKT)—to bring about, achieve, cause

These two similar-sounding words generate as much confusion as any two in the English language. As it happens, both words imply producing or bringing about a result, but there's a distinct difference between the two words. EFFECT is actually the stronger of the two words. You use it when you want to express the idea of direct involvement in the accomplishment of a result or when you want to suggest the successful outcome of the intended action. AFFECT, on the other hand, is a somewhat more passive word. We use it when we want to get across the idea of influencing behavior but not necessarily producing a specific result.

So it is that when you take a medication it may AFFECT your condition, that is, make you feel a little better. Or it may produce a quick recovery, in which case we can say that the medication EFFECTED a cure.

Similarly, a strike may AFFECT the workers by making it harder for them to make ends meet at home, but it may also EFFECT important changes in working conditions.

AFFECT

Word Link: INFLUENCE

Memory Key: A FACT (AFFECT) of political life is that you need INFLUENCE to raise campaign funds.

EFFECT

Word Link: RESULT

Memory Key: IF FACTors (EFFECT) fall into place for a political candidate, the RESULT is usually success.

PRESUMPTIVE ═══════════════════════════════
(pri ZUMP tiv)—based on probability or an assumption; supposed; presumption, providing grounds for reasonable opinion or belief

PRESUMPTUOUS ═══════════════════════════════
(pri ZUMP chew us)—arrogant; unduly confident; overbearing, domineering

PRESUMPTIVE and PRESUMPTUOUS are related words, both coming directly from the Latin presumere, "to anticipate, suppose, or take for granted," but as so often happens in word families, each has gone its own way.

You use the word PRESUMPTIVE to indicate a reasoned and well-founded basis for accepting something as true before it's actually proved. Political reporters will often talk in terms of PRE-SUMPTIVE indications that the Senate will pass a particular bill.

And if you are an heir PRESUMPTIVE, it means that you can legitimately dream of how you're going to spend your inheritance.

PRESUMPTUOUS, the better-known of the two words, suggests arrogance and overconfidence to the point of being offensive. "How can you be so PRESUMPTUOUS?" you might ask a person you know who suggests that he or she might do a better job of raising your children than you do.

PRESUMPTIVE

Word Link: ASSUME

Memory Key: If there's enough noise, you can ASSUME that the PRESENT HIVE (PRESUMPTIVE) of bees in your backyard is a big one.

PRESUMPTUOUS

Word Link: ARROGANT

Memory Key: It's ARROGANT to PRESUME TOO MUCH (PRESUMPTOUS) about other people.

Word Game [

Match the word on the left with its closest definition on the right.

1. appraise	A. to influence
2. apprise	B. a presentation
3. presentiment	C. to estimate
4. presentment	D. to bring about
5. effect	E. arrogant
6. affect	F. foreboding feeling
7. presumptive	G. to inform
8. presumptuous	H. believable
9. credible	I. praiseworthy
10. creditable	J. probable

Answers: 1-C 2-G 3-F 4-B 5-D 6-A 7-J 8-E 9-H 10-I

Word Game II

Fill in the blank with the word in this section that best fits the following sentences:

1. Through his patience and good judgment, the mediator was able to _____ a solution to the conflict underlying the strike.

2. The defendant was found not guilty because the jury found his story highly _____.

3. The politician's _____ manner offended many of the voters in his district.

4. Even though the team lost, the coach felt his players had given a _____ performance.

5. Weather is known to _____ the moods of many people.

6. A jeweler was called in to _____ the value of the diamond.

7. The jeweler was then asked to _____ the woman of the value of the gem.

8. The lawyer delivered his _____ to court with no emotion.

9. There is now _____ reason to expect an acquittal.

10. She stayed at home because she had a _____ about the trip.

Answers: 1. effect 2. credible 3. presumptuous 4. creditable 5. affect 6. appraise 7. apprise 8. presentment 9. presumptive 10. presentiment

Word Game III

On the left are the memory word links to each of the words in this section. Fill in the proper word.

1. trouble ahead _____
2. value _____
3. believe _____
4. inform _____
5. worthy _____
6. court _____
7. result _____
8. assume _____
9. influence _____
10. arrogant _____

Answers: 1. presentiment 2. appraise 3. credible 4. apprise
   5. creditable 6. presentment 7. effect 8. presumptive 9. affect
   10. presumptuous

MEMORY KEY REVIEW

See the picture of the memory key in your mind.

XV
Business as Usual
WEEK 3, DAY 3

The words in this section are no mere playthings. They are made out of sterner stuff. They have to do with the down-to-earth events affecting our daily lives. You may find that a <u>caveat</u> heeded at the right time protects your <u>equity.</u> And making a dubious pun, we know we aren't reading about home plate in baseball when a business writer tells us that our currency is being <u>debased</u> (di BASED). While the Irish wish us well by saying, "May the wind be always at your back," my wish for you is that the next mail will bring you a <u>fiscal</u> delight in the form of a <u>windfall.</u> You will find all the words in this section turning up frequently in the news. Make it your "business" to know them.

caveat
equity
mediate
proprietary
retroactive
windfall
embargo
fiscal
debase
usurious

CAVEAT

(KAV ee at)—a warning, caution, or admonition

CAVEAT comes directly from Latin, spelled the same way, where its meaning was "let him beware." You use the word when you want to give an added sense of officialdom or authority to cautionary advice. The phrase Smoking Can Be Harmful to Your Health is a CAVEAT that appears on every pack of cigarettes.

CAVEAT is frequently joined by yet another Latin word, EMPTOR. The Romans used the phrase CAVEAT EMPTOR, "let the buyer beware," whenever the seller of a product or a service had no obligation to the buyer once the money was paid and the product accepted. We use the term today in much the same way, although the phrase tricks some people into believing that the expression denotes a guarantee of sorts to the buyer. The saying can also be used in situations other than business. As the late James T. Farrell once wrote about the milieu of his novels, "It is a world in which the principle of CAVEAT EMPTOR applies recurrently in relationships of love, friendship, or family."

Word Link: BEWARE

Memory Key: A friend of yours has become ill as the result of a veal dish he ate at a certain restaurant. Veal, of course, is the meat from a calf. So BEWARE of the CALF-HE-ATE (CAVEAT).

EQUITY

(EQ wuh tee)—justness; value; stock

EQUITY has several meanings. We use it as a synonym for shares of stock in a company, and we also use it to describe the value of a property beyond the amount owed on it such as mortgages. A house worth $75,000 with a $20,000 mortgage has an EQUITY of $55,000. Most often, though, the word is used as a synonym for justness, fairness, and impartiality. A judge in a court of law should handle each of his cases with complete EQUITY.

Word Link: EQUAL

Memory Key: A friend has come over to your house for a visit and you're pouring a cup of tea. Your pot has only two cups left in it. You want to be fair and equal, so you pour EQUAL-TEE in each cup. You pour with EQUITY.

MEDIATE
(ME dee ate)—to attempt to reconcile; settle; arbitrate

Two of your close friends are no longer speaking to each other. You take it upon yourself to patch things up. You act as an unbiased go-between, a person with equal interest in each side of the quarrel. You act, in other words, as a MEDIATOR.

But now let's say that these two same friends are arguing over a specific point and you are called in to settle the argument. Both friends agree to abide by your decision. Now you are more than a MEDIATOR; you have become an arbitrator.

Though not synonymous, MEDIATE and arbitrate are similar in that both words imply the notion of acting as a nonpartisan go-between in order to settle a dispute between two or more persons. The difference, however, is in the amount of power you assume in this role. If you have no power to settle the argument, you are there simply to MEDIATE. If you have power, then you're there to arbitrate.

Word Link: BETWEEN

Memory Key: Associate a pile of MEAT YOU ATE (MEDIATE) with the shred of meat BETWEEN your teeth.

PROPRIETARY ════════════════════════════
(pruh PRY uh tar ee)—owned as private property; held under a patent, copyright, or trademark of a company

If you read the business section of a newspaper you may come across a news item that a pharmaceutical firm is introducing a new PROPRIETARY product, a product developed, owned, and patented by the firm. Anytime you own something privately you have a PROPRIETARY interest in it, as there can be a PROPRIETARY nursing home, a PROPRIETARY shoe store, and the like.

But just because you have a PROPRIETARY interest doesn't mean you will always act with propriety (pruh PRY uh tee), that is, with correctness, politeness, or conforming to accepted rules and customs. The two words, which some people confuse, have a common ancestor, proprius, "private or peculiar to oneself," which eventually came to mean property. The Latin split into two branches, one becoming our word PROPRIETARY (ownership) and the other one, propriety (correct behavior). Each day most of us observe the proprieties of our society.

Word Link: OWNERSHIP

Memory Key: To help fix the notion of OWNERSHIP, imagine yourself the owner of a house with excellent ventilation, in other words, a very AIRY house. You own PROPERTY that's AIRY (PROPRIETARY).

RETROACTIVE ════════════════════════════
(re tro AK tiv)—relating to past matters; effective as of a specified prior date; an increase in wages effective as of an earlier date

If you've ever been involved in a lengthy salary dispute, the word RETROACTIVE ought to be very familiar to you. The key to the word lies in the Latin prefix retro, "backward." If the raise you were granted was RETROACTIVE to January 1, it doesn't matter that you didn't agree to terms until April. You still get the higher wages from January to April.

While we're at it, the prefix retro turns up frequently in our language. When a museum or gallery features a retrospective of a painter's work, you can expect a look backward, a show of the painter's early work. And when a person's behavior is described to you as being retrogressive, you can be sure it's going from better to worse.

Word Link: BACK

Memory Key: On a tour of a nuclear laboratory, your guide warns you to stay well BACK of the RADIO-ACTIVE (RETROACTIVE) material.

WINDFALL
(WIND fall)—sudden profit or good fortune

After an autumn storm on our farm, the deer in our area will come to feed on the apples that the strong winds have knocked to the ground. The deer are enjoying, literally, a WINDFALL, a sudden burst of good fortune. We don't know for sure, but the word WIND-FALL may indeed owe its Old English origins to a similar reaping of fruit. We do know, however, that a WINDFALL doesn't neces-sarily benefit everybody. Why else would there be such a contro-versy surrounding the WINDFALL profits of the oil companies?

Word Link: SUDDEN WEALTH

Memory Key: If money grew on trees, you would have SUDDEN WEALTH from a WIND that makes the money leaves FALL (WINDFALL).

EMBARGO

(im BAR go)—an official prohibition or restriction of foreign trade by one or more nations against one or more other nations

Most Americans became introduced to the word EMBARGO under the not very pleasant circumstances of the Arab EMBARGO of oil shipments to the Western nations during the 1975 Arab-Israeli War. But you don't have to be an oil-producing nation to set up EMBARGOES. Our own country, for instance, had an EMBARGO against Havana cigars. What you have to remember about EMBARGO is that it can work both ways: A country can EMBARGO goods to a certain nation, that is, not permit the goods to go there. Or it can EMBARGO goods from a certain nation.

Word Link: PREVENT

Memory Key: Your normal shortcut through the neighbor's yard is blocked by a thick bar across the gate in the shape of the letter M. The M BAR PREVENTS you from GOing (EMBARGO).

FISCAL

(FIS kuhl)—financial; pertaining to the finances of a government, business, or institution

FISCAL is a word often used interchangeably with financial and monetary, but there are some subtle and telling differences between the three words. Financial is an umbrella-type word meant to cover all aspects of money management—everything from multimillion-dollar government budgets to your own struggling efforts to keep your checkbook in balance. Monetary is best reserved for situations that deal directly with the amount of dollars in circulation —with the minting of money and the like. This brings us to FISCAL, a more formal word than financial or monetary which is meant to be used in business and public treasury matters. The policy of the Federal Reserve Bank to keep interest rates high is more a FISCAL policy than a <u>financial</u> or <u>monetary</u> policy. And when the trustees of a foundation are negligent in money matters, let's accuse them of FISCAL irresponsibility, not <u>financial</u> irresponsibility.

<u>Word Link:</u> MONEY

<u>Memory Key:</u> A salmon who wanted to specialize in MONEY matters would go to a FISH SCHOOL (FISCAL) for accounting.

DEBASE ――――――――――――――――――――――――――
(di BASE)—to degrade or lower the intrinsic quality character or value of

DEBASE is a short word with a lot of punch and a word that, more than most, reflects some of the troubles of our age. Modern Cassandras claim—and, who knows, they may be right—that much of our life is being DEBASED. Inflation DEBASES our money each year. Sloppy word usage DEBASES our language. A confusion of values DEBASES our national character. Hopefully these arguments will themselves be DEBASED by future events in our society.

<u>Word Link:</u> LOWER

<u>Memory Key:</u> The only way to get a tall bass fiddle through a low door is to LOWER THE BASS (DEBASE) as you walk through.

USURIOUS ――――――――――――――――――――――――
(you ZOOR ee us)—pertaining to the charging of extremely high or unlawful interest on loaned money

It wasn't too long ago that anybody who was asking for interest rates of 15 and 16 percent on loaned money was accused of engaging in USURY, USURIOUS lending practices. Today, though, with interest rates higher than ever, there's nothing unusual about a 15 or 16 percent interest and therefore nothing unlawful or USURIOUS about such lending practices. Or is there? Only your local loan shark can tell you.

Word Link: HIGH INTEREST

Memory Key: One method of putting up collateral for a HIGH INTEREST loan would be to USE YOUR IOUS (USURIOUS). Good luck!

Word Game

Here are some definitions. Write in the correct word from this section.

1. relating to past matters   _____

2. to reconcile   _____

3. a warning   _____

4. held under ownership   _____

5. an official prohibition   _____

6. value   _____

7. financial   _____

8. exorbitant interest   _____

9. degrade   _____

10. sudden good fortune   _____

Answers: 1. retroactive 2. mediate 3. caveat 4. proprietary 5. embargo 6. equity 7. fiscal 8. usurious 9. debase 10. windfall

Word Game ⅠⅠ

Answer true or false to the following statements:

1. Usually, the longer you own your home, the more <u>equity</u> you amass.   _____

2. An oil <u>embargo</u> by a Middle Eastern country would mean more oil for the West.   _____

3. A treasurer has expertise in <u>fiscal</u> matters.   _____

4. A <u>retroactive</u> clause in a contract means that it takes effect at the moment of signing.   _____

5. You expect a loan shark to engage in <u>usurious</u> lending practices.   _____

6. A remodeling job is likely to <u>debase</u> the value of your property.   _____

7. A <u>caveat</u> is the same thing as a guarantee.   _____

8. If you own a car, you have a <u>proprietary</u> interest in keeping it in good shape.   _____

9. The best way to <u>mediate</u> an argument is to take sides immediately.   _____

10. You have a <u>windfall</u> from a lottery ticket you found unexpectedly.   _____

Answers: 1-T 2-F 3-T 4-F 5-T 6-F 7-F 8-T 9-F 10-T

Word Game III

Write the correct memory word link for the words below.

1. mediate _____
2. caveat_____
3. proprietary _____
4. embargo_____
5. debase _____
6. fiscal _____
7. retroactive _____
8. equity _____
9. usurious _____
10. windfall _____

Answers: 1. between 2. beware 3. ownership 4. prevent 5. lower
6. money 7. back 8. equal 9. high interest 10. sudden wealth

XVI

Heavy Hitters

WEEK 3, DAY 4

It's one thing to joke with someone, but something else to treat that person with <u>derision.</u> It's one thing to be forgetful, but something else to be <u>oblivious</u> to everything around you. It's one thing to be left out, but something else to be a <u>pariah.</u> Each of the words in this section will give you a way of expressing yourself more clearly and colorfully.

derision
oblivious
aloof
impasse
machination
nullify
epitome
recrimination
pariah
Byzantine

DERISION
(di RIZH un)—ridicule or scorn; mockery; contemptuous laughter

If you've ever been the object of DERISION, you probably don't recall the time with any fondness. Nobody, after all, likes to be laughed at. Indeed, as the Latin translation of DERISION indicates (the word combines the idea of <u>down</u> with the idea of <u>laughter</u>), it is the ultimate put-down.

<u>Word Link:</u> LAUGH DOWN (put down)

<u>Memory Key:</u> THE REASON (DERISION) people LAUGH DOWN is not always obvious.

OBLIVIOUS
(uh BLIV ee us)—not noticing; unaware; forgetful; inattentive

Understanding this word thoroughly might help you to be more tolerant in judging somebody who seems to be forgetful. An OBLIVIOUS person is forgetful and usually for a good reason: He or she is preoccupied with a problem, a worry, or an illness, and is consequently OBLIVIOUS of whatever is going on around him or her. On the other hand, OBLIVIOUS can be used in a less understanding context. Some people are so self-centered and callous, they are OBLIVIOUS of the feelings of others and their circumstances.

<u>Word Link:</u> UNAWARE

<u>Memory Key:</u> An apology you might make to someone whose feelings you've hurt: "O BELIEVE US (OBLIVIOUS), we were UNAWARE of your feelings on the subject."

ALOOF

(uh LOOF)—detached; reserved; cool or distant in manner

ALOOF is one of a number of words which owes its origins to Dutch sailing terms. (Others include yacht, leak, boom.) It comes from the Dutch word aloufe, which means "to head into the wind away from the shore." So when we describe a person as being ALOOF, we're saying that he or she prefers to "steer clear" of everyone. It's not necessarily a criticism: It's simply an observation having to do with that person's interaction with other people. A number of public figures, chief among them the late Charles de Gaulle, were known for their ALOOFness. They steered clear of close relationships.

Word Link: COOL TO PEOPLE

Memory Key: A LOAF (ALOOF) of bread kept in the refrigerator will be COOL to the PEOPLE who eat it.

IMPASSE

(IM pass)—deadlock; blind alley; difficulty offering no apparent solution

The last thing you want to arrive at whenever you're involved in any sort of negotiation or argument with somebody else is an IMPASSE. It means the two of you have reached a point at which neither of you is willing to yield another inch. The word comes to us unchanged from the French language, where it means "dead end."

Word Link: BLOCK

Memory Key: Whenever you come to a roadBLOCK, you know the street is IMPASSable (IMPASSE).

MACHINATION

(mack uh NAY shun)—secret plot; intrigue; crafty scheming; conspiracy.

The officer of a well-known publishing company gained controlling interest of his business not long ago through what a newspaper reporter called a series of MACHINATIONS. The reporter's choice of words suggests that this officer is not a person you would put your trust in, since MACHINATION stresses the idea of conspiratorial scheming and of activities that exceed the normal boundaries of legality.

Word Link: PLOT

Memory Key: The MECCA NATION (MACHINATION) of Saudi Arabia is frequently victimized by political PLOTS. (Mecca is one of the capitals of Saudi Arabia.)

NULLIFY

(NUL uh fy)—to make ineffective, useless, or valueless; cancel; invalidate; negate; void; abrogate; annul

NULLIFY, invalidate, negate, void, abrogate, annul are so similar in meaning that most of the time they are interchangeable, especially when used in a legal context. They all suggest that something is brought to an end.

But NULLIFY, like these other words, can be used in more than just a legal sense. You may have had a wage increase, but you find it has been NULLIFIED (canceled out) by inflation and taxes. Negate would be a reasonable substitute for it implies that one thing destroys another. You could also say that during the day sunlight NULLIFIES the light of the full moon.

Lawyers know that a false signature will NULLIFY a contract, but you could use invalidate or void just as well. Abrogate also means to NULLIFY, invalidate, or void, though it is used more often with formal agreements such as treaties. <u>Annul</u> tends to imply that no contract existed in the first place, as when a marriage is <u>annulled.</u>

<u>Word Link:</u> CANCEL OUT

<u>Memory Key:</u> A question to a lawyer: NOW IF I (NULLIFY) CANCEL the order, do I still have to pay for it?

EPITOME
(i PIT uh me)—embodiment; essence; a summary that is typical of the whole

Most dictionaries list as their primary meaning for EPITOME a faithful condensation or abridgment, but people tend to use the word to describe all of the qualities or characteristics of something or someone in a concentrated form. The Lord's Prayer is the EPITOME, in many ways, of the teachings of Jesus. It summarizes the teachings of Jesus. And there are people who behave in a way that is the EPITOME of a particular characteristic, as a miser is the EPITOME of greed.

<u>Word Link:</u> TYPICAL

<u>Memory Key:</u> O PITY ME (EPITOME) is a TYPICAL lyric in some sad songs.

RECRIMINATION
(re krim uh NAY shun)—a reply to an accuser by making a countercharge against him; retaliation

RECRIMINATION is a word most people have heard about but few use accurately. To treat it as a synonym for <u>accusation</u> is imprecise, because the essence of a RECRIMINATION is that someone is responding to an accusation with an accusation in return. In other words, before you can issue a RECRIMINATION, first you have to be the object of an accusation. Many arguments end up in mutual RECRIMINATIONS.

Word Link: RETALIATE

Memory Key: A war against crime is our country's way of RETALIATING against the CRIME IN the NATION (RECRIMINATION).

PARIAH ════════════════════════════════
(puh RY uh)—social outcast; someone despised or rejected; an exile or expatriate

One of the many consequences of the Watergate scandal was that Richard M. Nixon, shortly after he resigned from the presidency of the United States, became something of a PARIAH in his own country (an outsider, a social outcast). This word comes to us from India, where it was the name given to the largest of the lower castes in Southern India. The Indian word itself is derived from the word parai, "drum." The reason for the connection is that PARIAHS for centuries were the hereditary drum beaters during festivals.

Word Link: OUTSIDE

Memory Key: One way to cope with the problem of being locked OUTSIDE your house is to PRY A (PARIAH) window open with a screwdriver.

BYZANTINE ═══════════════════════════════
(BIZ'n teen)—intricate; complicated; devious

BYZANTINE, something of an international vogue word, is stray-
ing from its basic meaning. It comes from Byzantium, a city
founded in 660 B.C. and the present site of the city of Istanbul in
Turkey. The essence of BYZANTINE is a style of art and architecture developed during the Byzantine Empire between the fifth and
fifteenth centuries. Large domes, rounded arches, and elaborate
and colorful mosaics were the signature of this art form. In fact,
this is the only definition offered by most American dictionaries,
not intricate, complicated, or devious. But as new editions appear,
undoubtedly these meanings will be included.

"It (Byzantine) has become a fashionable put-down for political
and other activities of which one disapproves," writes lexicogra-
pher Laurence Urdang in the linguistic journal Verbatim. "I find it
useful. It is also an oversimplification and possibly unhistorical.
There was a great deal more to Byzantium than the complexity of
its politics."

Political writers seem fond of using the word to describe complex negotiations and maneuverings. A television commentator
described a lobbyist as "intimately familiar with the BYZANTINE
procedures involved in getting a piece of favorable legislation
through Congress." A reporter wrote: "Government bureaucracy
grows BYZANTINE in its complexity." I like this word because it
evokes the narrow, winding, mysterious streets where you can so
easily become lost in a Near Eastern city.

Word Link: COMPLICATED

Memory Key: Doing BUSINESS with TEENS (BYZANTINE) can
be COMPLICATED.

Word Game []

Find the word in this section that means the <u>opposite</u> of the following definitions:

1. breakthrough _____
2. alert _____
3. ratify or affirm _____
4. warm, concerned _____
5. insider _____
6. statement of support _____
7. respect _____
8. uncharacteristic of _____
9. simple _____
10. openness and honesty _____

Answers: 1. impasse 2. oblivious 3. nullify 4. aloof 5. pariah 6. recrimination 7. derision 8. epitome 9. Byzantine 10. machination

Word Game []

Fill in the blanks with the proper word from this section.

1. His divorce so upset his parents that he became a _____ _____ to his own family.

2. A mediator was introduced into the strike proceedings to break the _____.

3. Because the child dressed differently from everyone else, she was frequently the object of _____.

4. The man was so _____ to everything around him, he never heard the doorbell ring.

5. Once you make an accusation, you shouldn't be surprised at a series of _____ from the person you accused.

6. Political leaders in many countries are constantly wary of the _____ of their opponents.

7. People who are _____ are sometimes accused of being snobbish.

8. Most people consider a decathlon champion the _____ _____ of a competitive athlete.

9. The treaty was _____ because of certain intolerable conditions.

10. The _____ dealings in money markets are hard to understand.

Answers: 1. pariah 2. impasse 3. derision 4. oblivious 5. recriminations 6. machinations 7. aloof 8. epitome 9. nullified 10. Byzantine

Word Game ▯▯▯

Match the word links in the left-hand column with the correct words to the right, as you visualize the memory key.

1. typical	intricate
2. plot	derision
3. countercharge	epitome
4. outsider	impasse
5. block	machination
6. cool	recrimination
7. forget	aloof
8. laugh down	oblivious
9. nullify	cancel
10. Byzantine	pariah

Answers: 1. epitome 2. machination 3. recrimination 4. pariah 5. impasse 6. aloof 7. oblivious 8. derision 9. cancel 10. intricate

XVII

Mind Over Matter

Words with abstract meanings are usually tricky to learn and even trickier to master. It isn't enough to know the meaning of the word; you have to appreciate as well the subtleties involved in its use. Each of the words in this section relates to a mental state, an attitude, or a point of view. And each of them suffers from more than its share of misuse. Read the introductions carefully to get a grasp of the nuances.

empathy
ambivalent
bias
objective
opportunist
rationale
ingenuous
meretricious
transmogrify
euphoria

EMPATHY

(EM puh thee)—sympathy; the quality of fully sensing, understanding, and identifying with the feelings and thoughts of another person

Like so many words in the English language, EMPATHY is either blessed or cursed (depending upon your point of view) with an abundance of synonyms, among them pity, sympathy, compassion, and condolence. But EMPATHY carries a specific quality missing in these other words. It goes beyond pity, beyond sympathy, beyond compassion, and beyond condolence. It implies your ability to actually put yourself in the shoes or the skin of somebody you're feeling sympathy for.

Some people use the word interchangeably with commiseration, but here, too, there is a subtle difference. If you're at a lecture and you hear a speaker make an embarrassing blooper, you may commiserate with him, showing an immediate and spontaneous display of sympathy. But to demonstrate EMPATHY, you would have to know yourself what it's like to be in the same position.

Word Link: UNDERSTANDING SYMPATHY

Memory Key: It's easy to have SYMPATHY for a hungry person standing in front of an EMPATHY refrigerator.

AMBIVALENT

(am BIV uh lent)—simultaneously attracted to and repelled by an object, person, or the like; having mixed feelings

AMBIVALENT is made up of two Latin words, ambi, "soft," and valens, "strong," and the relationship between the two Latin terms fairly well explains the word's meaning. When you are AMBIVALENT about something, you're pulled strongly in two different directions. You're at a resort. The place is lovely and the weather is ideal, but the food is terrible. You don't know whether to leave or not: You're AMBIVALENT. You probably have people in your life whose combination of pleasant and unpleasant makes you AMBIVALENT toward them. You like them and you don't like them. I remember a woman once telling me about a man she knew: "I love him, but we're so different I could never marry him." That's AMBIVALENCE. Be careful not to confuse AMBIVALENT with ambiguous, a word we've already looked at (page 85).

Word Link: TWO WAYS

Memory Key: An early morning TWO-WAY financial transaction in the wilderness: At 2:00 A.M. a BEAVER LENT (AMBIVALENT) a possum ten dollars.

BIAS
(BY us)—prejudice; preference; an inclination for; a bent

This interesting word had its birth in the sixteenth century as, of all things, a bowling term. Bowling balls in those days were loaded on one side with lead so as to have them curve in a certain direction when they rolled. This was known as a BIAS. Over the centuries it acquired also the figurative sense of "leaning" in a certain direction for or against something.

Most of the time when we use this word we're conveying the notion of an opinion that really hasn't been reasoned out and isn't based on the facts at hand. Its meaning is close enough to prejudice so that much of the time the two words can be used interchangeably. Prejudice, however, carries a stronger feeling.

Word Link: PREJUDICE

Memory Key: It's hard to let the opinions of PREJUDICED people go BY US (BIAS) without calling them into question.

OBJECTIVE

(ob JEK tiv)—impartial; without bias; detached; impersonal; free from prejudice

OBJECTIVE is the opposite of our previous word, bias. To some people, the word suggests coldness or lack of feeling, but the essence of the word is that of having a fair and just view of things. If you look at a situation OBJECTIVELY, you're looking at the facts, such as they are, and not allowing any personal feelings or biases to color your thinking. Such an approach to life, of course, is better suited to some areas than others. Scientists, for instance, need OBJECTIVITY in their work, but too much OBJECTIVITY in your personal relationships could interfere with your ability to establish satisfying friendships.

Word Link: NEUTRAL

Memory Key: You are a juror and this is your first day in court. As you are NEW TO THE TRIAL (NEUTRAL) you want to be as fair as possible, taking no sides until you hear the evidence which is the OBJECTIVE of our legal system.

OPPORTUNIST

(op ur TOO nist)—someone who uses other people and every means possible to achieve what he wants, not caring if what he does is right or wrong

The ability to take advantage of opportunities as they arise is considered a virtue in our society. So it's curious, isn't it, that the personal noun so closely related to opportunity, OPPORTUNIST, should carry such an unsavory connotation. For an OPPORTUNIST is not just a person who takes advantage of opportunities, but a person who exploits situations and people for his or her own good without regard to moral considerations.

Word Link: ADVANTAGE SEEKER

Memory Key: Faust is an opera about a man who wants to get ahead in life so badly he makes a bargain with the devil. Think of an OPERA TUNE (OPPORTUNIST) about an ADVANTAGE SEEKER named Faust.

RATIONALE
(rash uh NAL)—justification; basis; logic; an explanation of the underlying reasons of one's belief, actions, etc.

The spelling of RATIONALE is so close to rational that at first glance it's easy to confuse the two words. To be rational means, of course, to be sensible, reasonable, and sound in your thinking. But a RATIONALE, a justification behind some action, doesn't necessarily have to embody these qualities. Indeed your RATIO-NALE for taking a particular action may seem quite irrational to somebody who doesn't share your view or doesn't understand your way of thinking.

Word Link: REASON

Memory Key: A ship captain's decision to RATION ALE (RATIO-NALE) was the main REASON behind the mutiny.

INGENUOUS
(in JEN you us)—sincere and frank; candid; naive; without guile; unsophisticated

An INGENUOUS person is open, apt to be warmly spontaneous, and often has the charming simplicity or gullibility of a child. I knew a quite famous man who in many ways was emotionally immature. Yet he admitted these shortcomings in such an INGENUOUS way

that you could never be angry at him because of them. The word
ingenue (ahn zhuh NEW) is a closely related word. In the theater
she is an actor who plays the part of an innocent, unworldly young
woman.

Occasionally people mistake the word for ingenious—the spelling difference is between an i and a u. This word, however, means
clever, inventive, or shrewd.

Word Link: GUILELESS

Memory Key: The trustful INJUN who KNEW US (INGENUOUS)
was GUILELESS.

MERETRICIOUS ━━━━━━━━━━━━━━━━━━━━━━━━
(mer uh TRISH us)—an artificial and tawdry attractiveness based
on pretense or insincerity; specious

Occasionally in English, two words with diametrically different
meanings share a common root. Meritorious and MERETRI-
CIOUS are two such words. They come from the Latin merere, "to
serve for hire," and each formed its own tree of meanings. One
grew to give us such words as meritorious, "praiseworthy," merit,
emeritus, etc. The other grew into meretrix, "prostitute," which
developed into our word MERETRICIOUS. The core meaning of
MERETRICIOUS is "deceitfully or artificially attractive." Why the
same root should produce words having such divergent meanings
is explained by Johnson O'Connor, who points out in his book
English Vocabulary Builder that the idea of "serving for hire," that
is, selling yourself, has sometimes been looked upon with scorn
and at other times with admiration.

In any event, MERETRICIOUS is a colorful word you can use
when you want to describe something in which, as semanticist S.
I. Hayakawa suggests, the "stress is on phony or trashy gim-
micks." During election time, for instance, you may find it interest-

ing to keep track of MERETRICIOUS campaign promises. And if you get bored during the speeches, you can read one of those mass paperback novels that make MERETRICIOUS use of sex to lure you into buying the book in the first place.

Word Link: FLASHY

Memory Key: If you want a FLASHY wedding, why not MARRY in a TREE HOUSE (MERETRICIOUS)?

TRANSMOGRIFY
(trans MAGH ruh fy)—to change completely; to transform in a grotesque, bizarre way

TRANSMOGRIFY describes a drastic change into something ugly, grotesque. In the spring of 1980, The New York Times used it to recount a situation in which toxic chemicals were dumped in a residential area called Love Canal: "The mothers of Love Canal awoke in the summer to find their little houses and gardens, which once seemed so safe, TRANSMOGRIFIED into poisonous places." You can use the word also in an abstract way. I read recently that an effective and workable clear air bill was TRANS-MOGRIFIED by legislation into a toothless monstrosity.

A number of other words implying change are sometimes used as equivalents of one another but should not be. Transmute stresses a fundamental change, usually from a lower to a higher state, as to transmute a nation of immigrants into a workable democracy. Transform means a basic change of the character of something. Energy can be transformed into power, or hate transformed into love. Metamorphosis also indicates a fundamental change in structure, but an almost magically induced one. We catch that sense in the metamorphosis of a larva into a butterfly. Transfigure is similar to transform, with the added element of a supernatural or religious feeling, usually in a positive and joyous sense. A mother's face is <u>transfigured</u> by love for her child.

<u>Word Link:</u> CHANGE

<u>Memory Key:</u> Imagine having to CHANGE a contact lens because a TRAIN's SMOKE WAS ROUGH on YOUR EYE (TRANSMO-GRIFY).

EUPHORIA ════════════════════════════════════
(you FOR ee uh)—having a sense of well-being and happiness

EUPHORIA is a blissful feeling that everything in your life is coming up roses. Usually the feeling comes when everything is going your way and you are supremely contented with your life. But sometimes the same feeling can come when there is no justification for it, when everything in your life is going down the drain. When this is the case, that is, when you are EUPHORIC about life in grim situations, the EUPHORIA is a symptom of a psychological disorder.

<u>Word Link:</u> JOY

<u>Memory Key:</u> When YOU FREE A (EUPHORIA) prisoner, he feels tremendous JOY.

Word Game

Write true or false next to the following statements:

1. You generally have <u>empathy</u> toward people you don't like. _____

2. <u>Opportunists</u> are usually <u>ingenuous.</u> _____

3. You might offer a <u>rationale</u> to someone who questions your actions. _____

4. It's easy to be <u>objective</u> when you're dealing with people you care about a great deal. _____

5. An <u>ingenuous</u> person is someone you have to be wary of. _____

6. A judge has a duty to discount whatever personal <u>bias</u> he or she may have in a case. _____

7. Reaching the top of a mountain after a difficult climb can be <u>euphoric.</u> _____

8. <u>Ambivalent</u> emotions can delay decisions. _____

9. There is a <u>meretricious</u> quality to an amusement park. _____

10. In Robert Louis Stevenson's story, good Dr. Jekyll was <u>transmogrified</u> into horrifying Dr. Hyde. _____

Answers: 1-F 2-F 3-T 4-F 5-F 6-T 7-T 8-T 9-T 10-T

Word Game 11

Write the correct word next to its definition.

1. an exploitative person _____
2. a prejudice _____
3. impartial _____
4. justification _____
5. guileless _____
6. sympathy _____
7. pulled two ways _____
8. false in a cheap way _____
9. a sense of well-being _____
10. changed for the worse _____

Answers: 1. opportunist 2. bias 3. objective 4. rationale 5. ingenuous 6. empathy 7. ambivalent 8. meretricious 9. euphoria
10. transmogrify

Word Game ⅢⅢ

Match the word links in the first column with the words from this section in the second column, and picture the memory key.

1. pulled two ways	A. opportunist
2. guileless	B. empathy
3. reason	C. ingenuous
4. prejudice	D. bias
5. advantage seeker	E. rationale
6. neutral	F. objective
7. understanding sympathy	G. ambivalent
8. happiness or joy	H. euphoria
9. tawdry	I. transmogrify
10. change	J. meretricious

Answers: 1-G 2-C 3-E 4-D 5-A 6-F 7-B 8-H 9-J 10-I

TEST III

You've studied fifty words by now, some of which are new to you. And you've reacquainted yourself with others. When you take this test, I'm sure you're going to be surprised and pleased by how many you know. Select the definition you believe is the correct answer. Go to the answer section following the test to check your results.

1. windfall A. a row of bushes and trees B. gale C. sudden profit
2. caveat A. warning B. a command C. usurpation
3. affect A. to conclude B. influence C. upset
4. pithy A. succinct B. tenacious C. witty
5. graphic A. poignant B. vivid C. constructive
6. creditable A. risky B. plausible C. deserving esteem
7. internecine A. stealthy B. mutually destructive C. international
8. mediate A. attempt to reconcile B. instruct C. demand
9. debase A. to unsettle B. degrade C. remove
10. tenuous A. slender B. tight C. indecisive
11. presentiment A. donation B. alarm C. premonition
12. equity A. credit B. value C. average
13. presumptuous A. hasty B. bombastic C. arrogant
14. retroactive relating to: A. rocketry B. past matters C. quiet
15. effect A. to regulate B. bring about C. modify

16. apprise A. to esteem B. inform C. seize
17. inexorable A. unpardonable B. crushing C. unyielding
18. credible A. believable B. superstitious C. gullible
19. proprietary A. self-centered B. privately owned C. respectable
20. cryptic A. hidden B. confused C. ancient
21. embargo A. license B. freight C. prohibition
22. presentment A. hunch B. presentation C. authorization
23. fiscal A. financial B. semiannual C. relating to insurance
24. aloof A. sociable B. high C. detached
25. empathy A. hostility B. sympathy C. fatigue
26. oblivious A. unaware B. shady C. devious
27. nullify A. to change B. question C. cancel
28. opportunist A. one who takes advantage of circumstances
    B. swindler C. modern artist
29. epitome A. proverb B. exact description C. essence
30. objective A. candid B. direct C. impartial
31. appraise A. to stare at B. notify C. estimate
32. mundane A. ordinary B. sophisticated C. dull
33. machination A. metal finishing B. plot C. stain
34. rationale A. allotment B. justification C. persuasion
35. cogent A. subtle B. compelling C. thoughtful
36. usurious pertaining to: A. practicality B. marriage C. interest
    rates
37. impasse A. consensus B. deadlock C. quandary
38. recrimination A. vindication B. recommitment C. counter-
    charge
39. ingenuous A. guileless B. inventive C. versatile
40. derision A. failure in duty B. ridicule C. act of throwing into
    disorder
41. bias A. preference B. fairness C. a common failing
42. presumptive A. insolent B. based on a probability C. decisive
43. pariah A. Hindu ruler B. social outcast C. diseased person
44. ambivalent A. pulled two ways B. sick C. hesitant
45. meretricious A. artificially attractive B. commendable
    C. wicked
46. Byzantine A. alluring B. cruel C. intricate

47. pejorative A. unhealthy B. making worse C. incriminating
48. transmogrify A. vanish B. change C. embarrass
49. obtuse A. dull B. stubborn C. sharp
50. euphoria A. sense of completion B. lovesickness C. well-being

Answers: 1-C 2-A 3-B 4-A 5-B 6-C 7-B 8-A 9-B 10-A 11-C 12-B
13-C 14-B 15-B 16-B 17-C 18-A 19-B 20-A 21-C 22-B 23-A
24-C 25-B 26-A 27-C 28-A 29-C 30-C 31-C 32-A 33-B 34-B
35-B 36-C 37-B 38-C 39-A 40-B 41-A 42-B 43-B 44-A 45-A
46-C 47-B 48-B 49-A 50-C

The benefit of a test such as this is that it shows you which words you will want to go back and review more carefully. The index at the end of the book gives the page on which the word appears. If you had 45–50 correct your score is exceptional. From 39–45 correct you have done well to excellent. A score of 30–39 correct means you have achieved a rating of fair to good.

XVIII

Measuring Sticks

WEEK 4, DAY 1

The only way your mind can make sense of the physical world surrounding you is to make distinctions relating to time and space. Consequently, we have a vocabulary of "measurement words." In one way or another these ten words describe or define limits. While we wait for the <u>millennium,</u> we humans muddle through our mundane <u>diurnal</u> schedules of minutes, hours, miles, and meters.

parameter
benchmark
chronological
imminent
evanescent
perennial
interstice
genesis
millennium
diurnal

PARAMETER

(puh RAM uh tur)—something used as a standard against which other things are measured

I have a sneaking suspicion that when many people use the word PARAMETER they are confusing it with perimeter, which means "the circumference or outer boundary of an area." There is an element of measurement within the definition of PARAMETER, but the words should not be used interchangeably. Basically a PARAMETER is a set of properties or qualities whose values determine the characteristics or behavior of a system. If this seems confusing, think of PARAMETER as a guideline or criterion. For example, the President of the United States establishes policy PARAMETERS (guidelines) within which various departments operate. In The New York Times, a writer uses the word in a more casual way: "By the PARAMETERS (criteria) that count, I am still among the more liberated women in my zip code."

Word Link: GUIDE

Memory Key: You go on a picture-taking expedition with a guide who carries two light meters. You call him that PAIR OF METERS (PARAMETER) GUIDE.

BENCHMARK

—fixed point of reference in measurement

To a surveyor, a BENCHMARK is a mark cut in some durable material such as a rock, cement post, or wall. It indicates an elevation reference point for a topographical survey. Outside surveying circles, the word can be used to denote a reference point in the measure of the quality or value of almost anything. In the wine industry, for instance, certain years are known as BENCHMARK years; these are the years whose wines serve as barometers by which to compare other wines. Movie critics frequently refer to certain films as BENCHMARK films, suggesting that these films have established new standards of excellence. In business, certain sales quotas serve as a BENCHMARK, a goal salesmen attempt to meet.

Word Link: REFERENCE

Memory Key: When you talk about a mark on a bench, you make a BENCHMARK REFERENCE.

CHRONOLOGICAL ————————————————
(kron oh LOJ i k'l)—in time sequence; arranged in order of time

Like people, words also have families and the grandfather of the word clan dealing with time is the Greek word chronos, "time, age." Chronos spawned such progeny as chronometer, "a clock of great accuracy," chronic, "lasting or coming back again and again," synchronize, "to cause to happen at the same time," anachronism, "a placement of something in a time when it was not known or did not exist," chronicle, "a record of events as they happened in time."
    We use the word CHRONOLOGICAL to refer to events or transactions arranged according to the order in which they happened. A sportswriter who writes a CHRONOLOGICAL history of football begins with the first recorded game. In a recent murder case, the defendant's lawyer pointed out the CHRONOLOGICAL impossibility of the suspect's having committed the crime. What he meant was that the defendant's sequence of activities made it impossible for him to be the murderer.

Word Link: SEQUENCE

Memory Key: If you have an orderly knowledge of crows, you have a CROW KNOWLEDGE (CHRONOLOGICAL) SEQUENCE.

IMMINENT

(IM uh nent)—impending; an ominous sense of something about to happen

Anytime you come face to face with the word IMMINENT, you know that something is about to happen. A sky blackened with clouds indicates an IMMINENT storm. Opposing troops massed on each side of a common border indicate that war might be IMMINENT. The root of this word is the Latin minari, "to project or overhang." There is an immediate sense of danger to IMMINENT, almost as if something is hanging over our heads about to drop. This something, however, doesn't necessarily have to be gloomy or bad. The birth of a child is IMMINENT once an expectant mother enters her ninth month of pregnancy.

A word sometimes confused with IMMINENT is immanent, "inherent or actually present in." To say, as some religious people do, that the Holy Spirit is immanent in their lives means that it's very much a part of their lives—and not about to happen.

Word Link: DUE ANY MINUTE

Memory Key: You're expecting a visit from the aunt of a friend of yours named Emma. In other words, EMMA'S AUNT (IMMINENT) is DUE ANY MINUTE.

EVANESCENT

(ev uh NES n't)—fleeting; ephemeral; lasting but a moment

EVANESCENT is a lovely, lyrical word that suggests delicacy and fragility. What makes something EVANESCENT? Mainly the fact that even though it vanishes almost as soon as it appears, it produces an immediate effect on us. Some sights, like the beauty of a rainbow, are EVANESCENT not only because they appear and vanish so quickly, but also because they catch us up momentarily in their beauty. The poet Robert Browning wrote about the

EVANESCENT glimpses of profound truth that come at different times, particularly in moments of contemplation.

Word Link: FLEETING

Memory Key: A woman wearing perfume sometimes leaves a FLEETING, HEAVEN SENT (EVANESCENT) fragrance as she passes.

PERENNIAL
(per EN ee ul)—perpetual; enduring; recurring regularly

A newspaper advertisement describes a particular dress style as "the PERENNIAL gem . . . one of those rare little dresses whose bloom refuses to wear off." This clever use of PERENNIAL not only conveys the idea of permanence, but it also links the word to its basic identification with nature in the description "bloom." Gardeners use PERENNIAL in reference to plants like the peony that come up year after year. But this suggestion of a continued recurrence in nature can be extended to anything else that seems to continue on in this fashion. We're all too well aware of the PERENNIAL economic cycles of growth and depression.

Word Link: OVER AND OVER

Memory Key: A great golfer can PAR ANY HOLE (PERENNIAL) OVER AND OVER.

INTERSTICE
(in TUR stis)—narrow space; crack; chink

Here's a word that's been around for a long time, although only recently it's become a noticeable part of our general vocabulary. It's a good word to use when you're talking or writing about any kind of space or gap, particularly a narrow one. Sweaters are made in various patterns and the INTERSTICES between the threads are of a different size in some than in others. When hiking in the mountains, you will often find flowers and even trees growing out of the INTERSTICES in the sheer sides of the cliff. And during a walk through a forest, you may see the blue sky through leafy INTERSTICES. The word is most often used with concrete objects, but it can be used imaginatively also with any open interval.

Word Link: OPENING

Memory Key: To ride most subways, first you have to put a token IN the TURN STYLE (INTERSTICE) OPENING.

GENESIS
(JEN uh sis)—the beginning or the creation of anything

GENESIS comes from genero, a Latin word meaning "give birth to or to produce" that is found usually either as a prefix or embedded elsewhere in a word in the form of gen. For example, GEN ESIS, the first chapter of the Bible, tells us of the birth of the world. Apparently the GENESIS of the universe had its origin in the "big bang." Using the word in a more mundane way, if you and I are talking about a local strike, you might explain to me that the GENESIS of the strike began with a dispute about a man who was fired from his job.

You might enjoy looking for gen in other words. A degenerate person has fallen from the position he had at birth. Gentlemen, geniuses, and generous people are all born that way.

Word Link: CREATION

Memory Key: A girl named JENNY SAYS (GENESIS) that the CREATION started with a bang.

MILLENNIUM

(muh LEN ee um)—a time of happiness, especially in the future

MILLENNIUM is a word with an upbeat message depicting a period in the future when there will be peace, an ideal government, and none of the old familiar ills and problems that hassle us. The word is frequently used as a symbol for utopia, an idealized place of perfection. Ironically, Adolf Hitler used the word in reference to the Third Reich, envisioning Germany's reign for 1000 years over the rest of the world.

MILLENNIUM comes from the Latin word mille, "a thousand," and originally referred to the 1000 years mentioned in the book of Revelation in the Bible concerning Christ's establishing the Kingdom of God on earth.

Word Link: 1000 YEARS

Memory Key: WILL ANY OF "THEM" (MILLENNIUM) ideas be alive in 1000 YEARS?

DIURNAL

(dye UR n'l)—daily; happening every day

During the excitement of the moon landing many of us learned that DIURNAL referred to anything that goes through a cycle of changes every twenty-four hours. Radio and TV commentators casually mentioned the DIURNAL path of the moon. Then, too, people who grow flowers know that some plants operate on a DIURNAL basis, opening their leaves during the day and folding them during the nocturnal (night) hours.

Another word having to do with daily events is quotidian (kwo TID ee un). It means something happening on an everyday basis, but stresses the fact that what is happening is ordinary and routine. Millions of commuters follow a quotidian schedule of catching a train or a bus to work each day at a certain time. It's not as esoteric a word as you may think.

Circadian (sir KA dee un) is yet another word dealing with daily time. This has to do with your bodily cycles. When you fly by jet from one coast to the other or to a foreign country, you will have a disruption of your circadian sleep patterns which results in the well-known "jet lag."

Word Link: DAILY

Memory Key: If you want different-colored nails each day of the week, you have to DYE YOUR NAILS (DIURNAL) DAILY.

Word Game

Match the words on the left with their definitions on the right:

1. interstice
2. benchmark
3. imminent
4. parameter
5. chronological
6. evanescent
7. perennial
8. genesis
9. millennium
10. diurnal

A. in time sequence
B. fleeting
C. guideline
D. fixed reference point
E. about to happen
F. narrow space
G. yearly
H. by day
I. beginning
J. a thousand years

Answers: 1-F 2-D 3-E 4-C 5-A 6-B 7-G 8-I 9-J 10-H

Word Game ⅠⅠ

Fill in the blanks.

1. A flower that grows every year is called a _____.

2. History books are usually written in _____ order.

3. Heavy clouds mean that a storm is _____.

4. Brief flashes of insight have an _____ quality.

5. Brain researchers are interested in the _____ between neural structures.

6. Babe Ruth's record of sixty home runs served as a _____ of power hitting for more than three decades.

7. Starting out on a new job, it's helpful to learn the _____ of responsibility.

8. The astronauts observed the earth's _____ patterns.

9. Some people believe the _____ will bring great happiness.

10. The _____ of our democracy was the American Revolution.

Answers: 1. perennial 2. chronological 3. imminent 4. evanescent 5. interstices 6. benchmark 7. parameters 8. diurnal 9. millennium 10. genesis

Review your memory keys.

Word Game ▯▯▯

Fill in the word after its word link.

1. opening _____
2. reference _____
3. guide _____
4. fleeting _____
5. sequence _____
6. over and over _____
7. due any minute _____
8. creation _____
9. 1000 years _____
10. daily _____

Answers: 1. interstice 2. benchmark 3. parameter 4. evanescent 5. chronological 6. perennial 7. imminent 8. genesis 9. millennium 10. diurnal

XIX
Diplomatic Missions

WEEK 4, DAY 2

Though you may never find yourself on a diplomatic mission in some far-off, exotic corner of the globe, each day newspapers, magazines, and TV newscasts report on these places. It's a fast-moving world you're living in, and your vocabulary has to keep up with it if you're going to be cosmopolitan and understand what's going on. These ten words will help.

indigenous
xenophobia
doctrinaire
sanction
imperialism
occidental
hegemony
démarche
cosmopolitan
geopolitics

INDIGENOUS

(in DIJ i nus)—originating in and characterizing a particular region

The trouble with INDIGENOUS is that most people use it interchangeably with native, even though the words have different implications. Native means having been born in a particular place, but INDIGENOUS means not only having been born in an area, but for all practical purposes having always been a natural part of that region. The starling is a bird now considered native to North America, but it is INDIGENOUS to England from where it was imported. While we normally refer to American Indians as being Native Americans, it would be more accurate to call them INDIGENOUS Americans, to differentiate them from we natives who were simply born here. Vermonters won't call you a native unless your family has lived in the state several generations. You can reply that though you may not be a native, they're not INDIGENOUS.

Word Link: ORIGINAL

Memory Key: IN DIG'IN around US (INDIGENOUS), we found the ORIGINAL site.

XENOPHOBIA

(zen oh FO bee uh)—fear or hatred of strangers, foreigners, or unfamiliar things

XENOPHOBIA is made up of two Greek elements, xenos, "stranger," and phobos, "fear." Curiously, though, the word was put together by the French, who have a historical distrust of strangers or foreigners. XENOPHOBIA is a strong word that portrays people with an irrational fear of something or somebody unfamiliar. The Soviet government, for instance, has long been XENOPHOBIC about foreign influences, and its XENOPHOBIA toward Americans is evident by the steps it takes to limit interaction between Soviet citizens and Americans. XENOPHOBIC can also be used to characterize individuals who choose to seclude themselves from the world, such as recluses. But don't be too quick to use XENO-PHOBIC interchangeably with misanthrope. A misanthrope is a person who hates everybody, whether they're strangers or not. But he does not necessarily fear them.

Word Link: FEAR

Memory Key: SEE NO FOE (XENOPHOBIA) is the kind of advice you might give to someone who FEARS his enemies.

DOCTRINAIRE
(dock truh NAIR)—dogmatic; dictatorial

This fascinating word is used mostly in a political context and describes a type of mind that knows what is best for you and me, and tries to jam it down our throats. DOCTRINAIRE expresses the intent of putting a theory or policy into effect regardless of its practicality or consequences. In France in 1815, DOCTRINAIRE was the name of a party or group that developed a doctrine to help reconcile two extreme political positions. But the members of the two opposing parties were contemptuous of the attempt, insisting the DOCTRINAIRE group had no practical understanding of the real issues.

A DOCTRINAIRE person usually gets locked into a rigid viewpoint, refusing to look at the actual circumstances. Humanity, as a whole, travels mostly in the center of the road of life and quite correctly is suspicious of DOCTRINAIRE theories that obviously are extremely foolish, or simply lack the balance wheel of common sense. The world faces DOCTRINAIRE Soviet communism. There is DOCTRINAIRE socialism as well as right-wing DOC-TRINAIRE capitalism. Every major religion contends with the dogmatic adherents of certain DOCTRINAIRE positions. Dogmatic is a good synonym: asserting something is true without proof and usually in a positive or arrogant way.

Word Link: DOGMATIC

Memory Key: A DOGMATIC physician on an airplane could be described as a DOGMATIC DOCTOR IN AIR (DOCTRINAIRE).

SANCTION

(SANK shun)—to approve authoritatively; permit. Also, coercive action taken by one country against another. To coerce is to force or compel by threats or violence.

What makes SANCTION so interesting is that used in one context it has to do with approval. In another the word changes character and becomes concerned with punitive measures.

Let's use it in the sense of giving approval. If you are a member of Congress and vote to SANCTION a multibillion-dollar program to develop synthetic fuels, you are agreeing to the expenditure of the money for that purpose. Or, if during a hockey game a fight breaks out and you tell your companion you don't SANCTION violence in sport, you're saying you don't approve, support, or encourage such fighting.

Using the word punitively now, if as a member of Congress you vote to impose SANCTIONS on a country, you're voting to punish that country for violating an international law or agreement by some form of restrictive action, such as cutting off trade or a blockade. The word SANCTION got a good workout during the Iranian crisis, when former President Carter ordered increasingly stiff SANCTIONS against the Iranian government to try to effect the release of the hostages. His measures were designed to hurt Iran politically and economically.

Word Link: APPROVE

<u>Memory Key:</u> The American colonists who SANK TEA ON (SANC-TION) on the eve of the Boston Tea Party are looked upon with APPROVAL.

IMPERIALISM ════════════════════════════
(im PEER ee uhl Iz'm)—having to do with building an empire; the extension of a nation's power and dominance by gaining political or economic control of other nations

IMPERIALISM means different things to different cultures and consequently cannot be reduced to a single meaning. When the Soviet government speaks of American IMPERIALISM, for example, it suggests an economic system that penetrates and controls, so as to subtly dominate different national world commercial markets. We see Soviet IMPERIALISM as having absolute military control with the concomitant economic and political subjugation of Eastern Europe, Afghanistan, and other nations. Interestingly enough, there was a time in the nineteenth century when to be called an IMPERIALISTIC nation was a compliment, for the term implied superior culture and energy. Today the word is always used negatively.

<u>Word Link:</u> EMPIRE BUILDING

<u>Memory Key:</u> Think of an emperor named Alfred who is building an empire. EMPEROR AL IS AN (IMPERIALISM) EMPIRE BUILDER.

OCCIDENTAL ════════════════════════════
(och suh DEN t'l)—of or belonging to the West

We speak of Japan as "the land of the rising sun" and refer to Far Eastern countries in general as the Orient, a word coming from the

Latin <u>orientis,</u> "rising." A Zen master said to me, "You speak of Japan as being in the Far East. We don't think of us in that way. But we do think of <u>you</u> as being in the Far West, 'the land of the setting sun.' " Now the Latin word for falling or setting (as the sun sets) is <u>occidentis,</u> so it is not accidental that Orientals think of us westerners as OCCIDENTALS.

<u>Word Link:</u> WESTERN

<u>Memory Key:</u> You could refer to an auto mishap in Arizona as a WESTERN OCCIDENT (OCCIDENTAL).

HEGEMONY ═══════════════════════════════
(hi JEM uh nee)—dominance or preponderant influence of one nation over others

HEGEMONY suggests domination and William Safire, in his book <u>Safire's Political Dictionary,</u> calls HEGEMONY a "dirty word for leadership." Quoting Edwin Newman, he says, "The Soviet and Chinese governments have a way of insulting each other that is peculiarly their own. 'You seek HEGEMONY,' the Chinese will tell the Russians. '<u>You</u> seek HEGEMONY,' the Russians will tell the Chinese. . . . Some of us on the outside thought that the two governments might be seeking HEGEMONY together." Actually, HEGEMONY is a close relative to <u>imperialism,</u> the difference being that <u>imperialism</u> is more of a philosophy or point of view while HEGEMONY is actually putting this point of view into practice. A current illustration of the word is Soviet Russia's HEGEMONY (dominance) over Eastern Europe.

<u>Word Link:</u> DOMINATE

<u>Memory Key:</u> The astrologer said that a HIGH GEMINI (HEGEMONY) in government will DOMINATE everyone else.

DÉMARCHE

(DAY marsh)—a change in plan of action or policy

DÉMARCHE, a French word meaning "a change of plan in action or policy," is used almost always in a diplomatic context. One of the principal criticisms of former President Carter's administration was the unexpected DÉMARCHES that occurred so frequently, confusing our relationships with other nations. The word also represents a diplomatic maneuver or a countermove by one or more nations in response to the actions taken by others. A report in the New York Review of Books stated that ". . . a joint DÉMARCHE by the United States, Britain, and the Soviet Union had undone a right-wing coup and restored a neutralist government to Cambodia." I find this sophisticated word provocative, because in a compact way it alludes to the machinations of diplomacy, a fact most of us outside of government often do not take into account.

Word Link: MANEUVER

Memory Key: The difficult MANEUVER on the DAY of the MARCH (DÉMARCHE) brought cheers.

COSMOPOLITAN

(koz mow POL uh tan)—worldly; universal; sophisticated

If you're COSMOPOLITAN, you probably feel at home almost anywhere in the world. You have an appreciation, or at least a broad tolerance, for the culture and habits of other societies, nations, and races. Your urbane approach to life comes from being widely traveled. Friends describe you as worldly and sophisticated. You have the COSMOPOLITAN characteristics of experienced diplomats and executives of multinational countries. These days many of us are becoming more COSMOPOLITAN partly through television's ability to reach into every area of the world, and partly because of the ease and speed of jet travel. It's appropriate that COSMOPOLITAN comes from the ancient Greek word <u>kosmopolites,</u> meaning "citizen of the world," for the Greeks had an insatiable curiosity about almost everything and traveled widely.

<u>Catholic</u> is another word embracing the idea of universality, of different people, places, periods, styles, and so forth. We hope you have <u>catholic</u> tastes in your reading selections.

<u>Word Link:</u> WORLD

<u>Memory Key:</u> A couple named COSMOS and POLLY TANNED (COSMOPOLITAN) themselves in every resort around the WORLD.

GEOPOLITICS
(gee oh POL it iks)—concerning the influence of physical environment on the politics of people

GEOPOLITICS, a word new to the twentieth century, is concerned with the interrelationship of politics and geography, that is, more specifically, the influence of geography on the political, economic, and demographic (study of population statistics) character of a country, particularly with regard to relations with other countries. Today geography determines the nature and scope of many worldwide trends and events. When certain nations have an abundance of vital commodities, while others have little or none, or when some nations are without food and are overpopulated, the geographical factors certainly have an impact on political realities. Former Secretary of State Henry Kissinger talked about what he called "the GEOPOLITICAL equation." He explained, "By this I mean the alignments and assessments that determine whether moderates friendly to us or radicals hostile to us dominate <u>key</u>

regions." GEOPOLITICS is one of the most important words of our times, for in it lies the fate of the world.

Word Link: GEOGRAPHIC

Memory Key: GEE, A POLITICAL (GEOPOLITICAL) GEOGRA-PHY class is interesting.

Word Game

Match the words on the left with the correct meaning on the right.

1. geopolitics	A. dogmatic
2. cosmopolitan	B. dominance
3. hegemony	C. of the west
4. occidental	D. fear of foreigners
5. imperialism	E. originating in
6. démarche	F. official approval
7. sanction	G. of the world
8. doctrinaire	H. empire building
9. xenophobia	I. politics as it relates to geography
10. indigenous	J. change of policy

Answers: 1-I 2-G 3-B 4-C 5-H 6-J 7-F 8-A 9-D 10-E

Word Game ⅠⅠ

Write true or false after each statement.

1. <u>Doctrinaire</u> people are usually flexible in their views. _____

2. Polar bears are <u>indigenous</u> to cold and snow environments. _____

3. If you <u>sanction</u> a particular view, you are probably opposed to it. _____

4. <u>Xenophobic</u> people are wary of strangers. _____

5. Paris can be described as a <u>cosmopolitan</u> city. _____

6. The Vietnamese War was an example of a struggle over <u>geopolitics</u>. _____

7. A country aggressively seeking to expand its influence throughout the world is frequently accused of being <u>imperialistic.</u> _____

8. The Soviet Union has enjoyed <u>hegemony</u> over eastern block nations since World War II. _____

9. China is an <u>occidental</u> country. _____

10. <u>Démarche</u> suggests inertia and inaction. _____

Answers: 1-F 2-T 3-F 4-T 5-T 6-T 7-T 8-T 9-F 10-F

Word Game 🎲

Write in the correct word next to its word link.

1. fear _____

2. western _____

3. original _____

4. approval _____

5. geography _____

6. maneuver _____

7. world _____

8. dominance _____

9. dictatorial _____

10. empire building _____

Answers: 1. xenophobia 2. occidental 3. indigenous 4. sanction
5. geopolitics 6. démarche 7. cosmopolitan 8. hegemony
9. doctrinaire 10. imperialism

XX

Military Aid

WEEK 4, DAY 3

The phrase "fighting words" conjures up an image of two guys about to square off against one another in a bar. However, though each of the words in this section is not related to a barroom brawl, all of them in their own way are "fighting words." The only time, though, you're apt to hear them mentioned in a bar is when somebody is discussing a military subject. The words have interesting backgrounds that will help you use them strategically.

junta
implacable
escalation
reprisal
surveillance
subjugate
deterrent
militia
infrastructure
coup

JUNTA

(HOON ta, JUN ta)—political clique; group ruling a country after seizing power by force

JUNTA, a Spanish word, is one of many foreign words that English has adopted as its own. There are differences of opinion as to how the word should be pronounced, with an h or a j. The American version, with a j, seems to be winning out. In any event, the word is used most often after a revolution or a political takeover, when a country is ruled by a committee of insiders who themselves plotted the change. JUNTAS, however, have a way of being overthrown themselves—by other JUNTAS.

Word Link: CLIQUE

Memory Key: People who HUNT TAgether (JUNTA) form a CLIQUE (small group).

IMPLACABLE

(im PLAK uh b'l)—unrelenting; inexorable; uncompromising

You sometimes hear government leaders described as being IM-PLACABLE, and I, for one, find such descriptions troublesome. I admire strong-minded people, but I worry about people who are IMPLACABLE. They are grim, relentless, merciless, and unyielding in their ideologies. You can also use IMPLACABLE in the description of places as well as people. Explorer Ernest Shackleton, for instance, found the Antarctic an IMPLACABLE adversary. He said it all!

Word Link: UNYIELDING

Memory Key: Scientists have been trying to come up with a tooth substance that would be UNYIELDING to the common tooth enemy, plaque (PLAK). Such an UNYIELDING substance could be called IMPLAKABLE (IMPLACABLE).

ESCALATION
(es kuh LAY shun)—an increase in extent, intensity, or scope

Escalators go up and down but ESCALATION is a one-way trip—up. First appearing in the late 1930s, ESCALATION became a buzzword during the Vietnamese War. You can apply the term to anything, but it's used most frequently in connection with prices or with a step-up in military activity. Many contracts have ESCALATION clauses designed to protect employees from rising prices. As prices go up, so do wages. Periodically, environmental groups gear themselves up for an ESCALATION of activity against nuclear energy.

Word Link: UP

Memory Key: To climb UP a very steep ninth hole, you have to SCALE A TEE ON (ESCALATION).

REPRISAL
(ri PRY s'l)—any act of retaliation, especially one of force or violence of one nation against another

There is no ambiguity to REPRISAL. It means doing to others what they've done to you, and worse if possible. The pattern in the Middle East over the past twenty years has been one of terrorist attack on Israel by Palestinians followed by REPRISALS by Israeli commandos against suspected Palestinian positions. But a REPRISAL can take many forms. Boycotts, blockades, the freezing of assets—these are all punitive measures frequently taken when one country is out to take revenge against another.

Word Link: REVENGE

Memory Key: Two stores are locked in a price war. One store, in
REVENGE, REPRICES A SALE (REPRISAL) item lower than cost.

SURVEILLANCE ════════════════════════════════
(sur VAY lans)—a close watch kept over a person or situation

It's one thing to keep your eye on somebody, and something else
again to keep somebody under SURVEILLANCE. SURVEIL-
LANCE has a feeling of intrigue and espionage about it. It has a
greater sense of urgency than to say you're simply observing
somebody. The police will keep a suspect in a crime under SUR-
VEILLANCE. Nations send up satellites whose function is to send
back SURVEILLANCE photographs of other nations. And a patient in an intensive care unit of a hospital would need something
more than observation; she'd need SURVEILLANCE.

Word Link: OBSERVE

Memory Key: If you look at an ant colony, you can OBSERVE
SERVILE ANTS (SURVEILLANCE).

SUBJUGATE ════════════════════════════════
(SUB juh gate)—to conquer or subdue

To be SUBJUGATED, figuratively, is to be put under the same
yoke that is put on oxen (Latin sub, "under", and jugum, "yoke").
In the days of Roman conquests, prisoners were required to crawl
under a yoke improvised of three crossed spears. The action was
a symbol of their SUBJUGATION. SUBJUGATION today retains
the meaning of conquering, enslaving, dominating, or controlling.
There was a time when Spain SUBJUGATED a large portion of

South America. Before the Civil War black people were under the SUBJUGATION of the owners of plantations. Extending the usage, you might say at times individuals do the unusual and SUBJUGATE their emotions to reason.

Word Link: CONQUER

Memory Key: Jughead, one of the characters from the comic strip "Archie," is known for his appetite. So the SUB (submarine sandwich) JUG ATE (SUBJUGATE) CONQUERED his appetite.

DETERRENT ════════════════════════════════════
(de TER ent)—prevention or restraint of action

DETERRENT comes from deter, which means "to prevent an action from taking place." Lately the word has been used almost exclusively in a military sense. In his book A Modern Guide to Synonyms, S. I. Hayakawa lumps DETERRENT with such military terms as armament, arsenal, munitions, ordnance, and weapons. Hayakawa also observes that both arsenal and DETERRENT have come into recent use in reference to a nation's nuclear arms. Arsenal used to mean simply a place where weapons were stored, but now it suggests a stockpile of nuclear warheads. So DETERRENT is something of a euphemism for a nuclear arsenal. The excuse many countries give for building up arsenals of nuclear weapons is that this stockpiling is a DETERRENT to war.

Word Link: PREVENT

Memory Key: Some people EAT HERON (DETERRENT) to PREVENT disease, a zany, unforgettable notion.

As you read the newspapers and listen to radio and TV commentators, you realize that military terms form an integral part of your daily vocabulary. So rather than concentrate on one word for today, I thought you'd be interested in a collection of terms.

MILITIA ══════════════════════════════════════
(muh LISH uh)—a citizen's army used at a time of emergency

A MILITIA is a body of citizens (as distinct from professional soldiers) trained for military purposes, but used only during times of emergency. Citizen members of the National Guard, navy, and Marine Corps comprise an organized MILITIA.

Word Link: CIVILIAN ARMY

Memory Key: Think of the MAIL ISSUED (MILITIA) to a CIVILIAN ARMY.

An ALLIANCE is a group of nations coming together to achieve some common objective that could not be accomplished by any of the nations singly. A principal military ALLIANCE is the North Atlantic Treaty Organization (NATO).

Word Link: CONFEDERATION

Memory Key: The NATO CONFEDERATION is the ALLIED AN-Swer (ALLIANCE) to the Soviet bloc.

COUNTERINSURGENCY by a government usually entails military and political operations against guerrilla forces who are inciting a rebellion. Insurgent means a rising up against established authority.

Word Link: AGAINST REBELLIONS

Memory Key: COUNT TERRY, IN SEARCH (COUNTERINSURGENCY) of guerrillas, was AGAINST REBELLION.

An INCURSION is a sudden, brief, and unexpected invasion.

Word Link: ATTACK

Memory Key: A rabbit who is ATTACKED and gobbled up suddenly by a dog finds himself IN a CUR'S (INCURSION) stomach.

INTERDICTION means "prohibition." In military terms, this is an action to prevent an enemy from using its forces or supplies by destroying it. In nuclear warfare, INTERDICTION forces would destroy enemy air or missile defenses.

Word Link: PROHIBITION

Memory Key: The bullet that went INTO DICK's SHIN (INTERDICTION) PROHIBITED him from running.

PARAMILITARY refers to an organized group that is not directly a part of a military force, but operates alongside of it. The members often perform nonmilitary activities in a war zone, such as giving medical care to civilians, aiding agricultural development, winning over the populace, and the like. Para is a Greek word meaning "alongside of."

Word Link: ALONGSIDE

Memory Key: ALONGSIDE the road were a PAIR OF MILITARY (PARAMILITARY) people.

INFRASTRUCTURE ═══════════════════════════
(IN fra struk chur)—a collective term for the subordinate or subsidiary parts of an organization, society, or undertaking

INFRASTRUCTURE is relatively new and, as you can see in the definition above, it has to do with the different elements that make up a whole. If you're talking about the INFRASTRUCTURE of a community, you mean schools, transportation, police and fire departments, roads, water supplies, and similarly related items.

INFRASTRUCTURE is used frequently as a military term, referring to the fixed installations that an armed force depends on. According to Robert E. Hunter in <u>Language of the Specialists</u> edited by Mario Pei, (Funk & Wagnalls, 1966), "INFRASTRUCTURE includes airfields, fuel dumps, communications systems, headquarters, supply depots. The word is taken from the French railroad term for the fixed parts of the railroad system, such as bridges, gradings, and tunnels. The development of INFRASTRUCTURE has been particularly important to NATO, where the ability to maintain, supply, move, and operate forces must be insured before the beginning of any European war."

INFRA in Latin means "below or beyond."

<u>Word Link:</u> FOUNDATION

<u>Memory Key:</u> The FOUNDATION of a house is put IN FOR THE STRUCTURE (INFRASTRUCTURE) to be built on.

COUP ═══
(coo)—a French word meaning a sudden, brilliant act or accomplishment; a masterstroke of strategy

COUP is the kind of word you'd use if you were tremendously impressed by a deal someone suddenly pulled off. A COUP can be done off the cuff or it can be the result of a lot of hard work swiftly brought to completion. Had former President Carter's desperate attempt to rescue the hostages from Iran succeeded, it would have been a memorable COUP, stunning the world. Metaphorically it would have been "a blow" for success, because the word comes from the Old French <u>couper,</u> "to hit someone or something hard."

COUP is used also in combination with other words. A COUP D'ETAT (<u>coup,</u> "a blow," <u>d'etat,</u> "to the state") is a sudden and illegal overthrow of a government by force. A COUP DE GRACE (a blow of mercy) is killing someone who is condemned or so mortally wounded it is kinder to "put him out of his misery." Usually it's done by a shot from a firearm. You can use the word figuratively as a finishing stroke, one that settles or puts an end to something once and for all. A smashing shot in a tennis game can give the COUP DE GRACE to the interminable rally.

<u>Word Link:</u> MASTERSTROKE

<u>Memory Key:</u> When the MASTER STROKES his pet pigeon it goes COO (COUP).

Word Game

Write true or false next to the following statements:

1. The United States has a long history of being <u>subjugated</u> by other countries. _____

2. <u>Surveillance</u> is now a routine part of military activity. _____

3. Terrorist raids almost invariably produce <u>reprisals</u> from the country affected. _____

4. A <u>coup d'etat</u> frequently puts a <u>junta</u> into power. _____

5. When military activity <u>escalates,</u> chances for peace become greater. _____

6. <u>Implacable</u> leaders are usually easy to deal with. _____

7. A weak military <u>infrastructure</u> in war can cause a sudden defeat. _____

8. The <u>militia</u> is usually a highly trained group of professional soldiers. _____

9. A large stockpile of weapons is thought to be a <u>deterrent</u> to war. _____

10. A <u>coup</u> is an unsuccessful attempt. _____

Answers: 1-F 2-T 3-T 4-T 5-F 6-F 7-T 8-F 9-T 10-F

Word Game ⑪

Match the word in the left-hand column with its synonym in the right-hand column.

1. junta	A. step-up
2. escalation	B. political clique
3. infrastructure	C. unrelenting
4. coup	D. act of retaliation
5. reprisal	E. spying
6. subjugate	F. prevention
7. deterrent	G. conquer
8. surveillance	H. masterstroke
9. militia	I. subordinate organization
10. implacable	J. citizen's army

Answers: 1-B 2-A 3-I 4-H 5-D 6-G 7-F 8-E 9-J 10-C

Word Game III

Write the correct word next to its word link.

1. prevent _____

2. revenge _____

3. up _____

4. clique _____

5. unyielding _____

6. observe _____

7. conquer _____

8. civilian army _____

9. masterstroke _____

10. foundation _____

Answers: 1. deterrent 2. reprisal 3. escalation 4. junta 5. implacable 6. surveillance 7. subjugate 8. militia 9. coup 10. infrastructure

XXI

Critic's Choice

When a movie critic describes the <u>protagonist</u> of a film as being <u>stereotyped</u> and goes on to characterize the script as being <u>redundant,</u> you suspect he didn't like the film. If you really understand what he's talking about and trust his judgment, you will probably take his advice and stay home. The words in today's section are ones you're likely to find in the arts section of your local newspaper. But none would be out of place in your everyday conversation.

protagonist
impresario
stereotyped
redundant
eclectic
euphemism
polemic
repertory
iconoclast
deus ex machina

PROTAGONIST

(pro TAG uh nist)—leading figure or figures in a drama or story

In fiction the PROTAGONIST is the character or characters central to the story. The subtlety of the word is that a PROTAGONIST doesn't always have to be just one person. It can be a group of people representing the same point of view. In John Steinbeck's novel The Pearl, the PROTAGONIST is the man Kino. But in his best-known book, The Grapes of Wrath, the Joad family is a plural PROTAGONIST, struggling against environmental and economic forces beyond their control. Going a step further, we can use PROTAGONIST to represent any leading figure or spokesman, supporter, advocate, or active participant in a cause. There are PROTAGONISTS for an economic system based on gold, PROTAGONISTS for fresher bagels, PROTAGONISTS for just about anything in the world.

Word Link: MAIN FIGURE

Memory Key: The MAIN FIGURE, a professional, on a tug o'war team might be called a PRO-TUGONIST (PROTAGONIST).

IMPRESARIO

(im pruh SAH ree oh)—manager or sponsor of entertainment such as a concert, opera, or special TV program

IMPRESARIO is a word we use primarily in reference to a person who puts together a performance or a tour of performing artists —singer, musicians, dancers, and the like. It's an arty word for "manager," which is precisely what IMPRESARIO means in Italian. The distinction between IMPRESARIO and manager has to do with the degree of involvement the person has with the tour or performance. To play it safe, you should reserve IMPRESARIO for a person whose skill in attracting publicity through his creativity, ingenuity, and other talents gets a performer universal recognition. One of the best-known IMPRESARIOS of this century was the flamboyant and unpredictable Sergei Pavlovich Diaghilev who is credited with having brought ballet into the modern world. Diaghilev discovered the legendary Nijinsky.

Word Link: MANAGE

Memory Key: The EMPRESS SAW RIO (IMPRESARIO), thanks to the Brazilian hotel MANAGER.

STEREOTYPED
(STER ee oh typed)—trite; conventional; without individuality; stale; dull

What makes STEREOTYPED interesting is that it comes from an old-fashioned printing term meaning "cast in metal from a mold." You could say that what is STEREOTYPED is taken out of a figurative mold. It's the same old thing used ad infinitum. Listen to how people speak and you'll notice many STEREOTYPED phrases such as "In our glorious past," "Onward and upward," "I point with pride." At one time these were refreshing, original metaphors but they lost their freshness and much of their meaning through overuse. They became trite, stale, and dull.

STEREOTYPED has a wide range of applications. Some books and plays have STEREOTYPED characters—characters with nothing original about them. They simply represent familiar types with no additional dimensions. It's all too easy to be lured into STEREOTYPED, shallow thinking when clichés form the basis of our ideas and observations.

Word Link: TRITE

Memory Key: The same old kind of music played on your stereo set is a TRITE STEREO TYPED (STEREOTYPED).

REDUNDANT

(re DUN dant)—wordy; repetitious

It's easy to be REDUNDANT. All you have to do is to repeat yourself over and over again. The origin of the word is the Latin unda, "wave." Therefore a REDUNDANCY is, in effect, "waves" of words that go on and on repetitiously. It means using more words than necessary to express your thoughts clearly and accurately and your listener's attention begins to wander. A woman described a horror film to me as being "all about an earthquake that was a disastrous catastrophe. It was just a terrible and dreadful series of disasters."

REDUNDANT and the adjective superfluous are not always interchangeable even though there is a close relationship. Superfluous applies to almost anything in excess, while REDUNDANT should be used within the boundaries of ideas, actions, or language.

Word Link: WORDY

Memory Key: A talkative aunt you've embarrassed might be called a WORDY REDDENED AUNT (REDUNDANT).

ECLECTIC

(e KLEK tic)—diverse; collected from various systems, sources, doctrines, and styles; broad

The core meaning of ECLECTIC is "selectivity," that is, choosing from different sources rather than depending on any one system or doctrine. If you have ECLECTIC tastes in eating, you aren't hung up on just one type of cuisine, but you enjoy food from many different traditions. The same analogy can be used with psychotherapists who've been exposed to different schools of psychological theory and take an ECLECTIC approach to therapy. An

ECLECTIC work of art represents different schools in one picture. Most of us have ECLECTIC preferences in our reading.

Word Link: COLLECTION

Memory Key: If you gathered together ticks who live in clay, you would have a COLLECTION OF CLAY TICKS (ECLECTIC).

EUPHEMISM ───────────────────────────────────
(YOU fuh mis'm)—an inoffensive expression; roundabout word in place of another one so as to avoid giving offense

Would you rather buy a "used car" or a car that's been "previously owned"? Would you rather be "fired" or learn that your job was being "phased out"? Practically speaking, of course, there's not much choice in either option, but one way of describing the situation <u>sounds</u> more palatable than the other, and we refer to such substitutions as EUPHEMISMS. Some people think of EUPHEM-ISMS as being evasive and insincere, but I like to think of them as a way of smoothing over the rougher edges. Writers often receive a rejection note saying, "Thank you for giving us the opportunity to see your work. We appreciate your interest in our publication." Now isn't that EUPHEMISM nicer than saying, "Your work is a mess. Face it, you're a lousy writer"? I'm for the right EUPHEMISM at the right time.

Word Link: SUBSTITUTE

Memory Key: UFOISM (EUPHEMISM) is a SUBSTITUTE way of describing flying saucer hysteria.

POLEMIC
(puh LEM ic)—argument against; controversy; attack on opposing ideas

Nearly every political statement, especially statements issued during election campaigns, is a POLEMIC to some degree—that is, an argument that aggressively attacks an opposing point of view or supports a particular belief, thus attacking the opposition.

A point to remember about POLEMIC is that the word does not refer to the validity of an argument. Forgetting for the moment whether you are right or wrong, the mere fact that you take a position strongly critical of the beliefs of somebody else makes you a POLEMICIST. The word cuts both ways since anybody who attacks you with words is a POLEMICIST as well. It's not unusual to hear a newspaper editorial referred to as a POLEMIC.

Word Link: ATTACK

Memory Key: A person critical of the reasoning behind a public opinion poll might ATTACK the POLL's AIM (POLEMIC).

REPERTORY
(REP ur tor ee)—theatrical company; stock collection

REPERTORY has several meanings, but the most familiar has to do with the theater. A REPERTORY company is a theater group consisting of a company of actors who work together as an ensemble, presenting different productions during the season. This is in contrast to a theater company that imports various actors and actresses for specific productions. There is a trend in the United States toward regional REPERTORY theaters. Such companies can be said to have a repertoire of plays they can produce. Repertoire can also be used in this manner in connection with orchestras or individual performers.

REPERTORY has applications outside the arts as well and works in virtually any situation in which you want to suggest a stock collection of something. Sportswriters consistently marvel over the REPERTORY of shots possessed by basketball stars.

Word Link: GROUP

Memory Key: A person chosen to represent a group of Tories, a political group in England, could be described as the GROUP REP for the TORIES (REPERTORY).

ICONOCLAST
(eye CON uh clast)—one who attacks traditional beliefs and customs

An ICONOCLAST is someone who attacks cherished or traditional customs, beliefs, ideals, or institutions. Usually, the rationale for such attacks is that all these things are either outdated, are based on superstition, or are just plain wrong—at least in the eyes of the ICONOCLAST. One of the most famous American ICONOCLASTS was Henry L. Mencken, a revered and influential journalist who used loaded words to dynamite more sacred cows than possibly any other writer in history. I knew of an artist, a crusty old ICONOCLAST, who preferred to have his pictures hang in a corner bar than in a museum.

Here's a bit of background on the word: An ICON is a painting of Christ, the Virgin, or of saints and is venerated extensively throughout the Greek Orthodox Church. In 726 A.D. the Byzantine Emperor Leo the Isaurian forbade the use of ICONS because he believed that images such as pictures and statues kept Jews and Muslims from converting to Christianity. His followers smashed all the ICONS they found. Not surprisingly they were called ICONOCLASTS, or image smashers.

Word Link: ATTACKING TRADITION

Memory Key: The man at the museum used A CAN OF GLASS (ICONOCLAST) to ATTACK the TRADITIONAL paintings.

DEUS EX MACHINA
(DAY us eks MACK uh nuh)—something introduced from the out-side to solve a problem

DEUS EX MACHINA is translated as "god from a machine" and dramatizes something that comes just in the nick of time to help us overcome a problem. You could look on it as a providential intervention.

The phrase refers to a device used by playwrights in ancient Greece. When a writer was stumped as to how to end his tragedy, he sometimes turned to a DEUS EX MACHINA to resolve his problem. This was a contraption rolled onto the stage, carrying someone impersonating a god high above the other actors. Since the Greeks believed that gods largely determined the destiny of the world anyway, they had no trouble accepting this one who wrapped up the evening's drama by dictating the fate of each of the characters. Occasionally even our good fiction writers are tempted to turn to a DEUS EX MACHINA to work out a plot.

I am sure that the secretary of the treasury, when wrestling with complex financial issues, secretly wishes for a DEUS EX MACHINA to roll into his life to resolve them.

Word Link: INTERVENE

Memory Key: DEE ASKS MAC IN A (DEUS EX MACHINA) soft voice to INTERVENE and solve her problems.

Word Game

Write S (for same) or O (for opposite) next to the following pairs of words:

1. redundant—succinct   ————
2. euphemism—substitute   ————
3. polemic—praise   ————
4. stereotyped—original   ————
5. eclectic—single approach   ————
6. impresario—promoter   ————
7. deus ex machina—artifice   ————
8. protagonist—minor character ————
9. repertory—collection   ————
10. iconoclast—worshiper   ————

Answers: 1-O 2-S 3-O 4-O 5-O 6-S 7-S 8-O 9-S 10-O

Word Game ⚅

Write true or false after the following statements:

1. Theater companies which recruit name actors and actresses for each performance are known as <u>repertory</u> companies. _____

2. Sex is a subject in which <u>euphemisms</u> are frequently used. _____

3. Good writers rely on the <u>deus ex machina</u> as a dramatic device. _____

4. Richard Nixon was the chief <u>protagonist</u> in the Watergate scandal. _____

5. The <u>impresario</u> has little to say about the workings of the company he or she is involved with. _____

6. <u>Redundancy</u> is a quality to be sought after in writing and speaking. _____

7. An artist may recognize different schools represented in an <u>eclectic</u> painting. _____

8. Politicians are usually happy when someone has written a <u>polemic</u> about them. _____

9. A play filled with <u>stereotyped</u> characters will introduce you to characters you've never seen before. _____

10. The <u>iconoclast</u> exposed the leaders of the new regime in his newspaper column. _____

Answers: 1-F 2-T 3-F 4-T 5-F 6-F 7-T 8-F 9-F 10-T

Word Game ▯▯▯

Match the word link on the left with the correct word on the right.

1. intervene	A. impresario
2. wordy	B. eclectic
3. attack	C. redundant
4. manager	D. repertory
5. copy	E. polemic
6. main figure	F. deus ex machina
7. substitute	G. euphemism
8. attacking tradition	H. stereotyped
9. group	I. protagonist
10. collection	J. iconoclast

Answers: 1-F 2-C 3-E 4-A 5-H 6-I 7-G 8-J 9-D 10-B

XXII

Power Potpourri

WEEK 4, DAY 5

Potpourri is a fancy way of saying a collection of unrelated items or a miscellany. Or, in other words, a mixed bag. That's what I'm handing you—a mixed bag of ear-catching words for your last day. Sprinkle them freely in your conversation and writing and watch your ideas grow.

rhetoric
pragmatic
equivocal
flabbergast
seminal
anomaly
prototype
forte
repudiate
magnanimous

RHETORIC ————————————————————
(RET uh rik)—showy use of words; insincere or pompous language

RHETORIC has fallen on hard times. In the days of Rome and through much of subsequent history RHETORIC meant the ability to use language eloquently to persuade and influence others. These days, however, the word suggests flamboyant, high-flown oratory without substance. William Safire, a longtime observer of the political scene, blames politicians like former Vice-President Spiro Agnew, whose words had more sound than content. In his book Safire's Political Dictionary, he wrote: "Rhetoric was associated with the expansive promises of the Kennedy and Johnson administrations and when delivery fell short of promise, emptiness insinuated itself into the definition of RHETORIC."

Word Link: HIGH-FLYING WORDS

Memory Key: A radar operator named Richard who is a specialist in HIGH-FLYING WORDS could be called RADAR RICK (RHETORIC).

PRAGMATIC ————————————————————
(prag MAT ic)—practical; realistic; judged by results

By all rights PRAGMATIC should be a neutral, perhaps even complimentary, word. PRAGMATIC people are those who deal with the way things are. They are practical, tough-minded, and realistic. In the sixteenth century, people used this word to describe somebody skilled in the day-to-day concerns of business. Yet today PRAGMATIC seems to be taking on a pejorative aura, particularly in the political arena. It now suggests a kind of unprincipled callousness. Former President Nixon is sometimes characterized today as having been a master of the PRAGMATIC arts of political maneuvering, but the characterization is not meant to be flattering.

Word Link: PRACTICAL

Memory Key: A mat made from rags that you used everyday could be called a PRACTICAL RAG MAT (PRAGMATIC).

EQUIVOCAL ——————————————————————
(i KWIV uh k'l)—ambiguous; of uncertain or questionable meaning or intent

The essence of EQUIVOCAL is ambiguity, having more than one meaning. The distinction, though, is that EQUIVOCAL suggests a deliberate type of ambiguity—an ambiguity meant to deceive and to create a false impression. You say one thing but mean another. For instance, a man I once worked for told me he'd received his Ph.D. diploma through the mail. From the way he talked, I thought that he'd not had the time to attend graduation ceremonies. Later I learned he'd bought a bogus Ph.D. certificate from a mail-order house. Now, he didn't actually lie to me. He did, after all, receive a Ph.D. certificate in the mail. But he'd led me to assume he'd taken a higher degree at a university, which is why his statement to me was EQUIVOCAL. If anybody has EQUIVOCATION down to a science, it's politicians. By being EQUIVOCAL they protect themselves from being pinned down to any single position.

Word Link: MISLEAD

Memory Key: The director misled the vocalist by cuing her at the wrong time. It was a MISLEADING CUE VOCAL (EQUIVOCAL).

FLABBERGAST
(FLAB ur gast)—to astonish or amaze

Part of the pleasure of talking comes from the sounds of words, and some are much more fun to roll off the tip of your tongue than others. Try FLABBERGAST. Say it to yourself. It's such a delightfully expressive word; to me the meaning and sound seem almost interwoven. FLABBERGAST is thought to come from a combination of flabby and aghast. Doesn't it seem to suggest vividly that you have become flabby and limp by being suddenly so dumbfounded or aghast by something you can hardly stand up? You are speechless with amazement. Once during a live radio game show the MC asked a contestant to name the arms of an octopus. Flustered, she replied, "Testicles," rather than "tentacles." The MC was so FLABBERGASTED that for a few seconds he couldn't think of anything to say and the audience erupted into shrieks of laughter. The Oxford English Dictionary tells us that FLABBERGASTED was first mentioned in 1772 as the latest thing in slang.

Word Link: ASTONISH

Memory Key: A fat labrador gassed (FLABBERGAST) up on beer to ASTONISH his master.

SEMINAL
(SEM uh n'l)—highly original

Knowing that SEMINAL comes from the Latin semen, "seed," gives a good clue to the meaning. A seed is an original source, so when you describe something, usually an idea, as SEMINAL, you're talking about something highly original. Einstein's theory of relativity can accurately be described as a SEMINAL idea—SEMINAL because entire concepts germinated from the idea. Any original source, whether an idea, a style, or whatever that strongly influences future developments, could be called SEMINAL.

Word Link: ORIGINAL

Memory Key: Like most Indians, a SEMINOLE (SEMINAL) was an ORIGINAL American.

ANOMALY ═══════════════════════════
(un NOM uh lee)—irregularity; abnormality; deviating from the normal order of things

Once when I was vacationing in the Deep South, there was a violent hailstorm. Since it almost never hails where I was visiting, the local newscaster described the storm as an ANOMALY. You use ANOMALY anytime you want to stress the idea of a deviation from the norm. Hail in Florida, a heat wave in Boston during the winter, a man wearing sneakers with a formal tuxedo, a professional basketball player who is smaller than six feet tall—these are all examples of ANOMALIES.

Word Link: EXCEPTION

Memory Key: A southerner making a change in his drinking routine might say, "AH NORMALLY (ANOMALY) don't drink on Sunday, but today ah'll make an EXCEPTION."

PROTOTYPE ═══════════════════════════
(PRO toe type)—original model; standard or typical example; archetype

PROTOTYPE is the word you use to describe the first or original model of anything—the model on which subsequent forms are based. A PROTOTYPE can be a piece of mechanical equipment, a person, or a group exemplifying a standard. One PROTOTYPE that changed the way we live was the airplane invented by the Wright brothers in 1906. The PROTOTYPE for epic poetry is generally thought to be Homer's <u>Odyssey.</u> And Roger Bacon, the thirteenth-century Englishman, is sometimes referred to as the PROTOTYPE of the modern scientist.

<u>Word Link:</u> MODEL

<u>Memory Key:</u> It takes a PRO TO TYPE (PROTOTYPE) a MODEL business letter.

FORTE
(fort)—strong point; whatever one does easily or well

All of us have something we do well—this is our FORTE, our strong point. And it's pronounced with a silent <u>e</u> as in <u>fort.</u> While discussing a ballet dancer, a critic said that her particular FORTE was the daring act. In football a tight end's FORTE might be his speed. And what a special treat to go to someone's home for a dinner whose FORTE is gourmet cooking!

FORTE began as a fencing term. It is the strongest part of the blade—between the middle and the hilt. The weakest is the foible —from the middle to the tip. A key strategy in olden days would be for you to receive your enemy's foible on your FORTE, a sound defense tactic. And who knows, his sword might shatter. So your opponent's foibles are his weak points, while your FORTE is your strong suit.

<u>Word Link:</u> STRONG

<u>Memory Link:</u> A STRONG FORT is tough to attack.

REPUDIATE
(re PYOU dee ate)—to reject or disclaim

To REPUDIATE is to refuse to acknowledge or to have anything to do with a person or thing. This is its general meaning. But if you have difficulty using the word, don't feel bad, as the general meaning of REPUDIATE overlaps in five different ways.

For example, let's say you want to explain that you reject something as having no authority or binding force on you. If you're running a business and you want to give your employees a pay raise, you might REPUDIATE the government's guidelines.

Or you have a fight with a relative and decide you don't want to have anything more to do with him. You REPUDIATE him as a member of the family. You have disowned him.

A third way to use REPUDIATE is when you want to reject an opinion, theory, statement, especially when you disapprove of it. Let's say a new theory has been proposed which you know absolutely is wrong. You REPUDIATE the idea as having no validity.

Another use is when you REPUDIATE an accusation or charge against you as untrue.

Finally, a government can REPUDIATE a debt. That is, it refuses to acknowledge that it owes anything to you or anyone else.

Word Link: REJECT

Memory Key: There ARE FEW DATES (REPUDIATE) the lawyer hasn't REJECTED.

MAGNANIMOUS
(mag NAN uh mus)—large-hearted, generous

What a word to stimulate the imagination! Over the years I've kept a relatively small list of words that have become favorites and this is one of them. It reminds me of the MAGNANIMOUS people I've met.

The noun form of the word, MAGNANIMITY (mag nuh NIM i tee), has a wonderful ring to it. Ernest Gordon of Princeton University told me how impressed he'd been as a boy growing up in Scotland by a preacher who used the word once in a sermon. " 'Oh, the marvelous MAGNANIMITY of the infinite love of God,' he said. It had a grand sound to it—the sound of majestic waves smashing themselves defiantly on black rocks; the sight of a great bens (Scottish mountain peaks) thrusting their assault into the curling white cumulus. MAGNANIMITY was and still is noble, big-spirited, generous, forgiving, free from vindictiveness or resentment, great-hearted, loving. . . . Sometimes the casuistry of my clever friends exhausts me and the cynicism of our political leaders depresses me. Then I hear that sound of the preacher's voice again, rolling out MAGNANIMITY as if it were the sound of a great choir of angels. MAGNANIMITY! Brave music plays in my soul again, stars shine, and my back stiffens. Yes, there is a great hope, because there is a great spirit."

This is the power of one word to inspire!

Word Link: GENEROUS

Memory Key: A MAGNUM of champagne I MUST (MAGNANI-MOUS) give to appear GENEROUS.

Word Game

Write true or false after each statement.

1. She was so <u>flabbergasted</u> by the announcement, she couldn't think of anything to say. _____

2. A <u>seminal</u> work is almost always plagiarized. _____

3. <u>Equivocal</u> statements are very clear in their purpose. _____

4. A dog with three legs is an example of an <u>anomaly.</u> _____

5. To <u>repudiate</u> a charge is to acknowledge its accuracy. _____

6. Verdi's <u>forte</u> was writing operas. _____

7. <u>Magnanimous</u> people are usually well liked. _____

8. <u>Rhetoric</u> is conversation filled with meaning. _____

9. <u>Pragmatic</u> people are usually result-oriented. _____

10. The model T Ford was a <u>prototype</u> of many cars to come. _____

Answers: 1-T 2-F 3-F 4-T 5-F 6-T 7-T 8-F 9-T 10-T

Word Game ▯▯

Match the word on the left with a word you might associate it with on the right.

1. magnanimous
2. rhetoric
3. pragmatic
4. equivocal
5. flabbergast
6. seminal
7. anomaly
8. forte
9. prototype
10. repudiate

A. speech
B. idea
C. model
D. realistic
E. shocking surprise
F. big hearted
G. specialty
H. vague
I. discredit
J. inconsistency

Answers: 1-F 2-A 3-D 4-H 5-E 6-B 7-J 8-G 9-C 10-I

Word Game ⅢⅡ

Write in the correct word after its word link.

1. reject _____

2. generous _____

3. original _____

4. exception _____

5. misleading _____

6. astonish _____

7. practical _____

8. strong _____

9. model _____

10. high-flying words _____

Answers: 1. repudiate 2. magnanimous 3. seminal 4. anomaly
    5. equivocal 6. flabbergast 7. pragmatic 8. forte 9. prototype
    10. rhetoric

TEST IV

Congratulations! This is the fourth and last test. You'd be amazed if you could see the activity these words are generating in your brain, how they are interrelated to other pieces of information, forging links from one area to another, expanding your knowledge in ways you cannot possibly conceive at the moment.

1. perennial A. early B. recurrent C. infrequent
2. junta A. emergency session B. political excursion C. political clique
3. eclectic A. brilliant B. diverse C. exciting
4. anomaly A. irregularity B. puzzle C. likeness
5. redundant A. heavy B. flowery C. wordy
6. prototype A. imitation B. original model C. mock-up
7. surveillance A. efficiency B. brief survey C. observance
8. impresario A. magician B. manager C. impersonator
9. doctrinaire A. dogmatic B. radical C. formal
10. evanescent A. fleeting B. sparkling C. colorful
11. benchmark A. exhibition B. label C. reference point
12. xenophobia A. zeal B. fear of strangers C. concern for health
13. pragmatic A. theoretical B. stubborn C. practical
14. imminent A. willing B. impending C. inevitable

15. occidental A. belonging to the East B. dark and shadowy C. belonging to the West
16. hegemony A. self-governing states B. mass migration C. dominance
17. stereotyped A. trite B. clear C. useless
18. equivocal A. fair-minded B. witty C. ambiguous
19. euphemism A. inoffensive expression B. praise C. cheerfulness
20. implacable A. dispassionate B. patient C. unrelenting
21. protagonist A. leading figure in story B. faultfinder C. opponent
22. flabbergast A. annoy B. astonish C. embarrass
23. parameter A. criterion B. outer limits C. occurring simultaneously
24. deterrent A. cleansing substance B. restraint of action C. defense
25. escalate A. dovetail B. increase C. compute
26. chronological A. in time sequence B. historical C. recurring periodically
27. seminal A. partial B. highly original C. controversial
28. polemic A. witty saying B. argument against C. outburst
29. subjugate A. conquer or subdue B. surrender C. consider carefully
30. interstice A. obstruction B. framework C. narrow space
31. reprisal A. surprise B. retaliation C. reward
32. indigenous A. originating in a particular area B. poor C. hardworking
33. imperialism A. regency rule B. empire building C. arrogance
34. rhetoric A. showy use of words B. philosophy C. repetition
35. millennium time of A. disaster B. impermanence C. happiness
36. démarche A. a traitorous act B. a humiliating demotion C. a change of plan of action or policy
37. cosmopolitan A. worldly B. bored C. immoral
38. genesis A. origin B. creativity C. phenomenon
39. diurnal A. long lasting B. daily C. pertaining to food

40. geopolitics A. the scene of politics B. world politics C. influence of the environment on the politics of people
41. iconoclast one who A. attacks traditional beliefs B. is an idealist C. is an individualist
42. infrastructure A. foundation B. partition C. buttress
43. coup A. clever retort B. small enclosure C. sudden brilliant act
44. sanction A. approve B. clean C. make holy
45. forte A. trait B. masterpiece C. strong point
46. repudiate A. answer back B. reject C. offend
47. repertory A. repetition B. stock collection C. stage
48. deus ex machina A. extensive cruelty B. outside intervention C. completely automatic robot
49. militia having to do with A. professional military force B. citizen's army C. guerrillas
50. magnanimous A. splendid B. optimistic C. large-hearted

Answers: 1-B 2-C 3-B 4-A 5-C 6-B 7-C 8-B 9-A 10-A 11-C 12-B 13-C 14-B 15-C 16-C 17-A 18-C 19-A 20-C 21-A 22-B 23-A 24-B 25-B 26-A 27-B 28-B 29-A 30-C 31-B 32-A 33-B 34-A 35-C 36-C 37-A 38-A 39-B 40-C 41-A 42-A 43-C 44-A 45-C 46-B 47-B 48-B 49-B 50-C

It's possible you haven't always done as well as you liked on these tests. Don't be discouraged, for you are already far ahead of where you were when you began. And remember that you are one of the comparatively few who have the tenacity to add to your vocabulary on a regular basis and the vision to know the many ways your life will be enriched by your efforts.

XXIII

25,000 Words in One Chapter

Whenever I think about the size of our language—over a million words—I'm always astonished. It's hard for me to conceive of that many. If you and I were alive when Shakespeare was writing his plays 400 years ago, we would be drawing on probably less than 100,000. Now we have ten times that number and more are being created daily. This explosive growth is the result of a surging tide of information that threatens to inundate us.

How then can you learn and remember even a fraction of the words that comprise your native tongue? Granted that using the memory keys in this book will help you to retain certain important words you really should know, what about the other ones that stump you as you read or listen?

When you're traveling with no recourse to a dictionary you have two choices: Either you skip the word and hope to remember to look it up later, or you try to puzzle it out. I happen to like this latter option best. Usually the overall meaning of a sentence or paragraph gives me a clue. Then I break down the word into its component parts. After I do this I make an educated guess at the meaning. It's a game that I and many other people enjoy playing.

To make this approach more fun, think of you and the word as having one feature in common: You both belong to a family. If you know my family, you also know something about me. And that's the way it is with words. As my father said, "Words don't just happen. They live and grow according to fixed laws; they are born and they die; they marry and have vast progenies."

Most of the words we know and use are grouped around certain word "families," known also as "roots." About 60 percent of these families or roots originated from Latin.

The family to which a word belongs forms the nucleus of meaning. But to understand the word fully you need to know some of the more common prefixes and suffixes. As you undoubtedly know, a prefix is an element such as anti-, semi-, or ad-, attached to the beginning of a word. A suffix is the end of a word: -ing, -ology, -ed, and the like. A prefix and suffix give the final clues to a word's meaning.

Let's pretend you're reading a medical article and come across the word congenital (the word appears in Chapter XI). For the sake of an example, let's assume you're not certain of the meaning.

You recall, however, that the element gen belongs to the Latin word genero, "give birth to, produce." So you know immediately that the word is going to have something to do with birth. The prefix con- ("with") confirms your feelings. The suffix -al simply indicates that some kind of action is going on, or is a result or condition. Having this information and studying the word in the context of the sentence, you deduce correctly that congenital means something existing at or from birth.

Knowing some of the more common prefixes and roots can possibly increase your reading vocabulary by 25,000 words, more or less. I know this seems like an amazing leap in your vocabulary. But a host of different words can be made out of the various elements combined together.

PREFIXES

Don't get thrown off when a prefix sometimes adds or drops a letter, such as ad- changing to ap- or at-. The change depends on the letter that follows in the rest of the word. For example, the prefix ob-, which means "toward, to, against, on, or before," often appears as oc-, of-, op-. Frequently a prefix will pick up and repeat the letter that follows: occupy, offend, oppose. I've indicated many of these different forms in parentheses. Also, when feasible I've included a word as an example of a particular usage.

AB- (a-, abs-) "from, away from, down"
    abhor, **a**vert, **abs**truse
AD- (ap-, at-) "to, toward"
    adapt, **ap**pear, **at**tract
AMBI- "around, both"
    ambiguous, **ambi**dextrous
ANTE- "before"
    anterior
ANTI- "against, opposed to"
    antibiotic
AUTO- "self"
    autobiography
BI- (bin-) "two"
    biannual, **bin**oculars
CATA- (cath-) "down, wholly, against, opposite"
    cataclysmic, **cath**ode
CIRCUM- "around, on all sides"
    circumlocution, **circum**vent
COM- (con-, col-, cor-, co-) "with, together, thoroughly"
    compatriot, **con**coct, **cor**respond, **co**eval
CONTRA- (counter-) "against, opposing, opposite"
    contraceptive, **counter**balance
DE- "down, down from, away"
    dehydrate, **de**cline
DIA- "through, across, between" A **dia**gnostician "knows" the difference "between" diseases.
    (**dia** and **gignosko**—"know")
DIS- (dif-, di-) "apart, away from"
    discern, **dif**ference, **di**lapidated
EX- (e-, ef-) "out, out of, from"
    exclusive, **e**ject, **ef**fervesce
HOMO- "same"
    homogeneous

IN- (im-, il-, ir-,) "in, into, on"
  inject, **im**itate, **il**luminate, **ir**radiate

IN- (im-, il-, ir-,) Here **in-** means "not."
  inhospitable, **il**legal, **ir**relevant

INTER- "between, among"
  international

INTRA- "inside, within."
  intramural

MAL- "bad, wrong"
  malpractice

MONOS- "one, simple"
  monogamous

NON- "not"
  nonsense

OB- "against, toward, on, before"
  obstacle, **ob**stetrics

PARA- "beside, near, beyond"
  parallel, **para**dise

PER- "thorough, thoroughly"
  percolate, **per**meate, **per**spective

POST- "after, behind"
  postscript

PRE- "before"
  predestination, **pre**requisite

PRO- "for, before, in place of"
  prostrate, **pro**fane, **pro**noun (used in the sense of in place of)

RE- "back, again, anew"
  recur, **re**call, **re**connaissance

SE- "separation, parting, privation, without"
  segregate, **se**cure (The Latin root **cur** means "care." Therefore **se**cure means "free from danger or care.")

SUB- (subter-, suc-, suf-, sup-, sus-) "under, below, subordinate, less than"
  submarine, **sub**terfuge, **suf**focate, **sup**press, **sus**pect

SUPER- "above, higher than, superior, more than"
  supernatural, **super**fluous

SYN- (syl-, sym-, sys-) "with, together"
  synergism, **syl**lable, **sym**phony, **sys**tematic

TECHNE- (techn-, tacho-) "an art"
  technology (also a root word as in pyro**technics**.)

TRANS- (tra-) "across, beyond, through, complete, surpassing"
  transatlantic, **trans**cribe, **tra**verse

UN- "not"
  unabashed, **un**believing

THE ROOTS OF YOUR WORD
FAMILIES

Here is your letter of introduction to some of the best-known Latin and Greek families in our English language.

CADA (cas, cis, cad, cid) "fall, cut, kill"
> cas**cade**, in**cis**ion, de**cad**ent, oc**cid**ent

CAPIO (cap, capt, cip, cep) "take, hold, seize"
> **cap**tivate, anti**cip**ate, re**cep**tacle

CEDO (ced, cess, ceed) "move, go, yield, withdraw
> re**cede**, re**cess**ion, pro**ceed**

CERNO (cern, cret, cert) "pick out, see as being different, separate"
> dis**cern**, se**cret**, **cert**itude

CHRONO "time"
> syn**chron**ize, **chrono**logical

CLAUDO (claus, clud, clus, clois) "shut, close"
> **claus**trophobia, con**clud**e, se**clus**ion, **clois**ter

CURRO (cur, curs, cour) "run, go"
> con**cur**, pre**curs**or, re**cour**se

DICO (dict, dex) "say"
> **dict**um, in**dex**

DUCO (duc, duct) "lead, take, bring"
> in**duc**e, ab**duct**

EQUUS (equ) "level, even, just, equal"
> If something is ad**equa**te it's "equal" to the job.

FACIO (fac, fic, fact, fect, fy) "do, make"
> **fac**simile, forti**fic**ation, **fac**totum, per**fect**, magni-**fy**

GENERO (gen) "give birth to"
> A de**gen**erate person has fallen "from" his position at "birth."

GRAPHO (graph, gram) "write, draw"
> epi**graph**, cardio**gram**

JACIO (jac, ject) "throw, cast"
> ad**jac**ent, inter**ject**ion

KOSMEO (cosmo) "order, arrange"
> **Cosmo**politan. In Greek **kosmos** means perfectly

arranged and therefore represents the word or universe.

LOQUOR (loqu) "say, speak, talk"

loquacious, soli**loqu**y

MANUS (manu, mani, man) "hand"

manuscript, **mani**fest, e**man**cipate

MITTO (mit, mis) "send, let go"

re**mit,** ad**mis**sible

PHONE "sound"

mega**phone**

PLICO (plicat, plicit, ply, plic, plex) "fold, twist, bend"

com**plic**ate, im**plic**t, com**ply,** ap**plic**ation, com**plex**

POLY "many"

polygamist, **poly**glot

SALIO (sal) "leap, jump"

A **sal**ient fact "jumps" out at you.

SCRIBO (scrip, script) "write"

pre**scri**be, post**script**

SEQUOR (sequ, secut) "follow"

sequel, per**secut**e, non **sequi**tur

SPECIO (spec, spic, spect, speculat) "see, look at"

specify, per**spic**acity, circum**spect, speculat**ion

TENDO (tend, tens, tent) "stretch, strain, thin, weak"

por**tend, tens**ion, pre**tent**ious

TESTOR (test) "bear witness"

To at**test** to the truth is to "bear witness" to it.

VENIO (ven, vent) "come"

re**ven**ue, con**vent**ion

VIDEO (vid, vis) "see, look, provide"

pro**vid**ent. Tele**vis**ion is something that we "see" from "far away" (**tele-**).

A formidable list? Maybe at the first run-through. But it's not really as intimidating as it looks. If you review the list occasionally, you'll find your eye picking up the components more easily and you will begin to be able to separate them out of unfamiliar words. Gradually you'll become more and more adept.

By the way, nearly every major dictionary produces a paperback version. I find they fit easily into a briefcase or a woman's pocketbook. It's a help when you're away from home and stumped on a word's meaning.

XXIV
Where Do You Go from Here?

You've just finished working with some of the most vital words of our age. They are high-powered and expressive, dealing with ideas, concepts, relationships, descriptions, and explanations. Being able to use them automatically broadens your intellectual horizons.

I've had two goals for you: First of all, I wanted the words you worked with to become second nature to you. My second equally important goal has been to try to kindle or rekindle your interest in words.

You may have felt at one time that adding to your vocabulary was a tedious chore and the only reason you worked at it was for the pragmatic purpose of increasing your chances of success, knowing that vocabulary will give you a significant edge.

But my hope is that <u>Word Memory Power in 30 Days</u> has persuaded you that words are not only important in your life, but can also be a source of pleasure. The more enjoyment you take in a word, the easier time you are going to have drawing it from your memory. If you have this sense of the rich possibilities in a word, then building a vocabulary can be fun.

I hope you will want to continue to add to your store of words. I myself am always on the outlook for new ones. I circle them in books. I tear them out of newspapers and periodicals. I write them down when I hear them on radio and TV. If I don't have a dictionary handy, I try to puzzle out their meanings. Later, I write each word on a three- by five-inch card, giving the pronunciation, the origin —which, incidentally, can be helpful in making up a memory key —and the various meanings. Invariably I write down the sentence in which it was used.

The next and most important step is to <u>use</u> the word. There's no substitute for this practice. Use it frequently in the beginning and you won't have trouble recalling it later on.

There's a simple game you can play which will strengthen your vocabulary in unexpected ways. As you read advertisements, sometimes use a substitute for the main words. For example, I came across an ad that said: "Americans discovered living colors." Is <u>living</u> the best word? Americans might also have discerned <u>vivid</u> or <u>vibrant</u> colors. Play the same kind of game when you pass by billboards as you walk along the street or are in a car or bus. This practice with synonyms is a great way to stretch your vocabulary. Did I say a <u>great</u> way? Why not <u>excellent,</u> <u>splendid,</u> <u>outstanding,</u> <u>nonpareil?</u>

You will need a good dictionary. Avoid the bargain basement ones promoted in come-on advertisements and supermarkets. Most of them are worthless. You pay somewhat more for the better ones, but they are worth every penny. One caveat about the names of dictionaries: The name <u>Webster</u> is generic. That means it is not a trademark and so anyone can publish a <u>Webster</u>'s dictionary. As it happens, there are two fine dictionaries using the name, <u>Merriam</u> <u>Webster</u> and <u>Webster's</u> <u>New</u> <u>World</u> <u>Dictionary.</u> Other equally fine ones are published by Random House, American Heritage, Funk & Wagnalls, Doubleday, Scribner's, and an excellent new one, the <u>Oxford American Dictionary.</u> And, of course, there is the nonpareil <u>Oxford English Dictionary.</u> Most of these publishing houses also put out paperback editions.

One further suggestion: Treat yourself to a dictionary of synonyms and a thesaurus as well. Both represent an efficient way for you to experiment with the wide range of possibilities to express yourself. English, more than any other language, abounds in synonyms, and you will find a vast array of words ready for you to use.

Keep in mind that your word supply will not grow unless you make up your mind to nourish it. Today, of all times, you need to have a quality vocabulary, for this is an age of words. The world is alive with them as they pour into our lives through radio and television, mass paperbacks, newspapers, and periodicals.

Words, whether we like it or not, are the principal forces in our lives. By them we go to war, search for peace, control inflation, learn our professions, acquire friends, give comfort, receive advice. The more you are the master of words the more control you will have over your life.

INDEX

INDEX

G

H

I